HIGH-ACHIEVING SECOND-GENERATION NIGERIANS IN THE UNITED STATES

Navigating Multi-Contexts to Success

Patricia Ngozi Anekwe

Naijaimprints@gmail.com

P.O. Box 228, Stratford, CT 06615

Library of Congress Cataloging-in-Publication Data

Anekwe, Patricia N.

High-Achieving Second-Generation Nigerians in the United States:

Navigating Multi-Contexts to Success

First Edition. Paperback 2021

Library of Congress Control Number: 2020925782

ISBN: 978-1-7363699-0-6

1. Nigerian-Americans—Second-generation—Academic achievement

2. Minority education—Black immigrants—Cultural Studies

3. Sociology—Immigrant education—Black studies

To maintain anonymity of the participants, I have altered some details without changing the essence of the message.

Naija Imprints (NIP) logo design by Chika Anekwe

Printed in the United States of America

In memory of Patricia Mary-Camel Attah-Onodu, Robert U. Attah, and Pius D. Anekwe.

For my children: Tobenna, Chika, and Amaka and all second-generation Nigerian-Americans.

For my granddaughter: Kola-Adaora.

To my second-generation nieces and nephews in college and graduate school—Ashley, Bryan, Didi, Chidi, Onyinyechi, Kevin, Emeka, and Will, I am proud of you for all you have accomplished and hope to accomplish as you pursue your dreams and passion in medicine, NFL, international relations, law, and fields yet unknown and explored.

To my younger second-generation nieces and nephews—Jide, Odera, Robert, Derek, Naeto, Olisa, Ryan, Gianna, Deborah, and Riley, you have great role models and excellent footprints to follow, and I know you will fulfill your dreams in the future. I am excited about your future and cannot wait to see where your passion leads you.

Table of Contents

Acknowledgments

This book is the result of my doctoral dissertation. Earning a doctorate was a desire from the seeds sown by my aunt Patricia Mary-Carmel and my father Robert Attah. As the first woman to earn a diploma in our town of Aku in Enugu State, Nigeria early in the twentieth century, Aunt Patricia Mary-Carmel subsequently sent my dad to school and he ultimately educated his children. My mother Victoria, with limited education, encouraged me to do well in school and taught me the value of education for women. My husband Clem has always been my greatest cheerleader and supporter. He provided moral and practical support, with plenty of encouragement along the way. His critical eyes and editing skills were invaluable for this project. My three children— Tobenna, Chika, and Amaka have always been the greatest source of inspiration for my work and their ongoing encouragement helped to make this dream a reality. Without the second-generation youth and the Nigerian women who participated in my study, there would not be a book. They are an incredibly resilient group of people, and I am indebted to them for their willingness to share their stories. Our stories are important and must be told.

Without the self-quarantine and isolation due to the COVID-19 pandemic, I am not sure that I would have had the same dedication to make this book a reality. The boredom of being home with little to do following my retirement in June of 2019 kicked off my desire to stop procrastinating. I had no more excuses after my retirement.

Finally, I thank my readers. My daughter Chika was my first reader and editor. Her help and encouragement were immeasurable. I know that I can always count on you, Ada Anekwe, and you have never disappointed me. Between working during the pandemic, house hunting, and moving and getting married, you delivered. I am indebted to you. My son Tobenna helped with some of the proofreading and I am grateful to him. My daughter Amaka and granddaughter Kola cheered me on with facetime chats. I also thank my high-achieving second-generation nieces Ashley, Didi, and Chidi for their input. Ashley, a graduate of Johns Hopkins and a medical student at Northwestern University, was excited about this book and shared some of her experiences and feedback. She affirmed some of my findings. Didi, a senior at Princeton, and Chidi, the valedictorian of her 2020 high school class, and a freshman at Yale, were equally excited to read through the draft and offered feedback. You all are part of my motivation for writing this book. I am immensely proud of all your accomplishments and I encourage you to follow your dreams.

The Prompt

An unexpected email on May 5, 2020, from Western Connecticut State University, my alma mater, was the sign and impetus to make my dream of this book a reality. I had always harbored the dream of turning my dissertation into a book and had always mused to myself that when I reached an arbitrary number of five hundred downloads from any one of the online depositories where my dissertation was available, I would begin writing in earnest about the incredible young people I first interviewed for the work in 2007. These students and their parents had so much to say about their experiences navigating American schools. By the time I sat down and began writing on May 17, 2020, I had reached 508 downloads from the WestCollections digitalcommons@WCSU since the paper had been posted there in June 2017. A few weeks later, I received an update informing me of "101 new downloads" during May 2020. This refueled my energy to keep writing. In July, as I was procrastinating on my next steps after I had completed the first draft, I received another update about 257 new downloads in June 2020 for a total of 871, and I eagerly went back to work on the revision of the first draft based on the feedback from my husband. In August, I received an update about 95 new downloads in the month of July for a total of 968 across the world, covering every continent except Antarctica. In September as I waited for my editor to review the manuscript, I received another update about 66 additional downloads in August, bringing the total to 1024 across 55 countries and 65 institutions. By end of December, it had exceeded 1200 downloads in 81 institutions. These notifications kept me surging ahead.

Introduction

Many of us have seen versions of the following recurring headlines in the news and national media during recent years in the United States:

"High school senior becomes first black valedictorian with school's highest GPA ever."[1]

ABC News (May 14, 2020), about Timi Adelakun, Class of 2020.

"Chaminade High School senior accepted to all eight Ivy League."[2]

Newsday (April 6, 2017), about Jude Okonkwo, Class of 2017.

"New Jersey teen accepted into all 8 Ivy League schools."[3]

ABC News (April 5, 2017), about Ifeoma White-Thorpe, Class of 2017.

"Prince George's County Student Accepted to 14 Colleges."[4]

NBC News (April 7, 2017), about Olawunmi Akinlemibola, Class of 2017.

"Augusta Uwamanzu-Nna picks Harvard."[5]

Newsday, (May 2, 2016), about Elmont Memorial High School valedictorian Augusta Uwamanzu-Nna, Class of 2016.

"Brockton High Student gets into 7 Ivy League."[6]

Boston Globe (April 27, 2016), about Obinna Igbokwe, Class of 2016.

"New York teen Harold Ekeh gets accepted to all eight Ivy League Schools."[7]

NBC News (April 7, 2015), about Harold Ekeh, Class of 2015.

What do the above headlines and others have in common? They describe children of Nigerian immigrants in the United States. These are members of an immigrant group who are supposedly not welcome to this nation because they hail from an undesirable country (Dawsey, 2018). As a Nigerian immigrant of forty years in the United States, a parent of three children born in the United States who have collectively earned seven Ivy League degrees, and a retired public-school educator with more than three decades experience in teaching and leading in an urban school, I hold dear to my heart the research that gave birth to this book. The second-generation young people whom I interviewed have many things in common with the students of the headlines above. For the study, "second-generation Nigerian" refers to children born in the United States to Nigerian immigrants and children born in Nigeria or outside Nigeria to Nigerian parents who migrated to the United States before the age of six.

Collectively and individually, Nigerian immigrants to the United States and their children believe that they can achieve academic success, and nothing will get between them and their goals. Parental messages of "can do" are consistently reinforced by relatives, family friends, and the community at large at every point of contact and opportunity. These adults consistently communicate the importance of education, hard work, and work ethics to second-generation children. As one second-generation participant in the study put it, "not achieving is not an option." Second-generation Nigerians in the United States have internalized the belief that they can achieve their academic goals and find strategies to navigate the various social, economic, personal, and other barriers they face.

CHAPTER 1

The Researcher and the Research

Top colleges take more Blacks, but which ones?[1]

New York Times, June 24, 2004

Several factors and many of the experiences of the researcher precipitated this study. It is important for readers to gain insight into the world of the researcher to better understand the context of the study, as the researcher is part of the lens through which to view qualitative research (Li, 2004). Some of the pertinent information relating to this researcher is mentioned below, as the book and research came as a culmination of several factors.

I am a Nigerian immigrant. I began my career as a public-school educator in a large urban New England school district in 1986, where I started as a substitute teacher and later spent more than three decades as a teacher, department leader, and assistant principal and then as director of a high-performing magnet high school in the same district. During those years, I had the opportunity to work with all types of students while raising my three children, who later went on to earn a collective seven Ivy League undergraduate and graduate degrees, including a Harvard Doctor of Science, and a medical degree from the University of Connecticut. I was always curious about why some of my students achieved and why some seemingly capable individuals failed to achieve. To me, it was clearly not an issue of race, as I also witnessed some white and Asian students who did not achieve in school as well as some brilliant African-American students who performed well. Entering a doctoral program in 2003 provided me with the opportunity to resolve some of my uncertainties.

My observations during my career, observations of Nigerian immigrants, and interactions with other immigrants clearly demonstrated to me that children could come from the same family and end up with different educational outcomes. I had witnessed this among some of my students of all races and ethnicities, including a few Nigerian families. As an educator, I observed that students who excelled in school had parental support, but I also witnessed students who excelled with minimal or no parental support and despite multiple challenges. As a result, I began to ponder the possibility of multiple variables that work to make students successful in school. That curiosity led me to enroll in the alpha cohort of a doctoral program in education at Western Connecticut State University in 2003.

When I began exploring topics for my dissertation in 2006, my intent was to study the educational experiences of second-generation Nigerian youth in America. However, circumstances led me to narrow my focus to the high-achieving ones. As a Nigerian immigrant, the researcher belongs to several Nigerian civic groups. Being a Nigerian, an educator, and a mother of high-achieving second-generation Nigerian youth provided me access to many Nigerian parents and youth at different locations and events. Some parents were so excited about the study that they volunteered their children for the study. When I sent out my surveys and met with some second-generation Nigerian youth at various places including Nigerian associations, conventions, and at a 2006 reunion of second-generation Nigerian youth in Atlanta, Georgia, those willing to participate in the study were those who perceived themselves as doing well in school and had the time to devote to the interviews. Having high-achieving second-generation children who have attended Ivy League colleges was also helpful in recruiting for the study. Due to logistical problems, study criteria, and time limitations, some youth were not able to participate in the interview process after completing the surveys. Being an in-group member eased my access to high-achieving youth, but it could have been a deterrent for the underachievers. Once I decided to focus on high-achieving individuals, participants were vetted according to the criteria detailed below. Each youth participant received a T-shirt with a "second-generation Nigerian" logo imprint as seen on the front cover of this book.

In addition to a doctorate in education, I hold BS and MS Degrees in sociology. I have conducted an ethnographic study of the childbearing patterns of Nigerian women in the United States as part of the requirements for a master's degree in sociology. I am also from one of the major ethnic groups in Nigeria, the Igbo, which is why most of the participants, both youth and mothers, are from the Igbo group. The Igbo group is one of the groups in Nigeria that is known to be achievement-oriented (LeVine, 1966).

As a Nigerian immigrant and a parent who has raised three grown children in the United States, I am privy to certain mores and have insights into the Nigerian culture that I brought to the study. On the other hand, I might have some biases that I could have introduced into the study. To overcome such biases, I was transparent in the sample selection, data collection, and analysis procedures. The use of triangulation of data sources and methods (surveys, in-depth youth and parent interviews, and a focus-group interview) was utilized to minimize the insider effects and biases on this study.

Youth for in-depth interviews were selected because they demonstrated that they were high achievers based on the following self-reported criteria:

1. High school cumulative grade point average of 3.5 or higher

2. High school class rank in the top 10%

3. High school AP courses undertaken (three or more) where available

4. Extra-curricular activities (high school and/or college)

5. High standardized test scores (SAT of 1200 or higher out of 1600, or 1800 or higher out of 2400, or an ACT score of 27 or higher)

6. College attendance and type of college

7. Awards and honors (High school and/or college)

8. College and career aspirations

Although these are some of the characteristics of high-achieving students, all the criteria did not need to be present for a youth to be invited to participate in the in-depth interviews. However, those invited for the in-depth interview had to meet a minimum of four of the criteria, and the higher the number of variables that were present, the more likely a youth was to be invited to participate in the study. Youth with unusual circumstances (one-parent household, attendance at an urban public high school, which are often underfunded) who scored below the stated guidelines were included to broaden the sample and the experiences of high-achieving second-generation Nigerian youth.

Therefore, samples selected for the study not only reflect a history of achievement as evidenced from respondents' self-report on the surveys but also incorporated the potential for academic success based on respondents' unique circumstances as evidenced from the survey responses. Including participants who have a diverse range of backgrounds and experiences increased the possibility of formulating a comprehensive understanding of the multiple factors that influence academic achievements for second-generation Nigerian youth.

All the youth invited for the in-depth interview described themselves as high academic achievers and ranked themselves in the top 10% of their high school class, including some valedictorians. Other than self-reports from the surveys, evidence of academic achievement was not verified for high school students in the study. Youth who were currently attending or who attended elite and Ivy League colleges were deemed as achievers, as an entrance to such colleges was deemed as sufficient evidence of academic achievement. That was also true of the focus-group interview that was conducted among high-achieving second-generation Nigerian youth attending an Ivy League college. Participants in this study volunteered and made themselves available for interviews.

Another reason I was drawn to this research topic was that the issue of high academic achievement of Black immigrant children has entered the national discourse as shown from the research of Massey et al., (2007). The *New York Times* headline at the beginning of this chapter ("Top colleges take more Blacks, but which ones?") caught my eyes and further ignited my interest in studying the children of Nigerian immigrants. Recently, high-achieving second-generation Nigerian youth have been getting media attention as shown in my introduction, yet there is a dearth of research on their educational experiences in the United States (Anekwe, 2008). As an immigrant from Nigeria and a public-school educator in the largest urban school district in a New England state, I had also grown leery of the narratives of black underachievement and was always curious to study how the children of Nigerians navigate the educational terrain in American schools. I had seen firsthand both high-achieving and low- achieving Black students amongst both second-generation Blacks as well as native-born Blacks (African or Black Americans with non-immigrant parents) in America and yearned to learn more about what determines their academic trajectories and outcomes. While researchers have focused extensively on underachievement amongst Black Americans, little research exists on the academic achievement of Black immigrant students and even less on the children of African immigrants. I was unable to locate any studies on second-generation Nigerian high achievers in the United States when I initiated this research in 2006. The research I subsequently conducted informs this book.

The qualitative case study used a multidisciplinary approach (surveys, in-depth interviews of youth and mothers, as well as a focus-group interview) with data triangulation from youth aged fourteen to twenty-five years as well as parents, to examine the academic experiences of high-achieving second-generation Nigerian youth. The project has since evolved into a longitudinal study of the youth participants to determine whether they had met their academic and career aspirations thirteen years later. Eleven high-achieving second-generation Nigerian youth were selected from the 106 youth who had earlier completed a survey about their demographic and academic information. Six college students participated in a focus-group interview and six parents (mothers) participated in an in-depth interview. All interviews were tape-recorded and transcribed. The qualitative software HyperResearch was used for data analysis after coding. Data analysis was guided by the research questions. The research was an attempt to answer the following three questions:

1. What are the characteristics of high-achieving second-generation Nigerian immigrant youth in the United States?

2. What are the effects of personal, family, school, and community factors on the academic achievement of high-achieving second-generation Nigerian youth?

3. What challenges do high-achieving second-generation Nigerian youth face in schools and how do they deal with the challenges of being Black, of immigrant origin, and high-achieving?

General Description of the Participants

As previously noted, eleven high-achieving second-generation Nigerian youth between the ages of fourteen and twenty-five years participated in the in-depth interviews. All the participants in the in-depth interviews were born to two Nigerian-born immigrants, thus forming what is termed as the second-generation. "Second-generation" refers to the children of immigrants (Zhou, 1997). These children are also known as American-born children of foreign-born parents (Kao & Tienda, 1995). For the purposes of this study, second-generation refers to children born in the United States to Nigerian immigrants and children born in Nigeria or abroad who emigrated before the age of six. Nine of the youth were born in the United States, whereas two were born in the United Kingdom and immigrated to the United States before the age of six. Seven youth participants were from the Igbo ethnic group and four were from the Yoruba group. There were three males and eight females. Five participants were in high school and five were college students. One participant was a graduate student.

Two of the high school participants were seniors at the time of the interview and have been accepted into elite colleges. One senior, who graduated as the valedictorian of her senior class after the interview, enrolled at an Ivy League college upon her graduation. Three other participants were valedictorians of their high school senior classes. The oldest participant had recently received a graduate degree in management from an Ivy League college. Four of the college students were attending an Ivy League college, and three of them were siblings with each other. The other college youth was enrolled in a competitive non-Ivy league private elite college in New England. The siblings were the oldest of more than five children [exact number omitted by design]. Apart from one participant with five siblings, the rest of the participants, including the focus-group had two or three siblings. The inclusion of multiple siblings from the same family enabled the researcher to examine how youth from a large family and from the same family experience education.

Three of the high school students attended an urban magnet high school, while the other two started in the same urban setting but later attended a suburban high school because their parents bought homes in the suburbs. Four of the college-age participants lived in an urban area and one lived in a suburban town and graduated from a public high school. Four of the college-age participants attended a Catholic high school. The lone graduate student attended an elite Catholic high school. All the participants grew up in two-parent homes. Nine participants grew up in New England. One grew up in a mid-Atlantic state and one grew up on the West Coast. Youth participants chose a pseudonym for the study or had one assigned to them, based on the researcher's discretion and interview transcriptions, however, all pseudonyms have been removed for the book to maintain the anonymity of the youth and parents.

Six Nigerian mothers participated in the parent interviews. All of them had resided in the United States for ten years or longer in 2007 when interviews were conducted, while three of them had resided there for more than 28 years as of 2007. Four parents were from the Igbo ethnic group and the other two were from the Yoruba group. Parent participants were college graduates and working mothers except for one, a stay-at-home mom of four then pursuing a graduate degree. One of the working mothers has a master's degree and has completed all the requirements for a doctoral degree, except the dissertation. Every mother interviewed had a child who participated in the in-depth interview study. Of the six mothers interviewed, two had multiple children in the study. Apart from two youth, all youth participants' mothers in the in-depth interviews were interviewed. All the parent participants resided in the New England area. Distance did not permit the inclusion of two parents. Parents were identified and linked to their children.

The focus-group participants, consisting of two males and four females, were students attending one of the top three Ivy League colleges in the United States. They ranged in age from eighteen to twenty-three years and grew up in the New England, Mid-Atlantic, Midwest, and West Coast regions. Their inclusion added geographical diversity of experiences to the study. All focus-group participants were born in the United States to both Nigerian parents except for one, who had a Nigerian father and a white mother. He explained that his mother convinced his dad to relocate to Nigeria when he was younger to shelter them from the bruises of racism and he relishes the experiences of having lived in Nigeria for a few years, calling upon it for a coping mechanism when needed. The two males were seniors and the females ranged from college freshmen to juniors. Two of the females were of the Yoruba ethnic group, whereas the other four students were of the Igbo ethnic group, including the two males. All focus-group participants completed their schooling [grades1-12] in the United States, except for one who spent a year abroad with his parents during his middle school years. The one participant who spent his early childhood in Nigeria returned to the United States at the age of six. The males were the last in birth order while the females were first.

Theoretical Underpinnings for the Achievement Patterns of Immigrant and Minority Students

Cultural Ecological Theory

One of the leading scholars on immigrant and minority education happens to be a first-generation Nigerian anthropologist, the late Professor John Ogbu. Theories of immigrant and minority education often focus on the cultural discontinuity/difference theory (Ogbu, 1982), also known as the cultural deprivation theory and the cultural ecological theory (Ogbu, 1987), but rarely on social cognitive theory (Bandura, 2001). Proponents of the cultural discontinuity theory believe that immigrant youth are at a disadvantage in their schooling experiences due to cultural, language, and interactional conflicts between the home and the school, therefore resulting in poor academic outcomes for minority children (Jacob & Jordan, 1987). Those who subscribe to the cultural discontinuity theory also believe that the longer the duration of residence in the United States and the more acculturated or assimilated to American society and norm, the greater the educational attainment of the immigrant children. This is also considered the straight-line assimilation (Gordon, 1964; Park, 1928) through which immigrants attain social and economic mobility across generations as they leave their ethnic enclaves for mainstream society, as was the case for earlier European immigrants.

The cultural difference perspective on minority education argues that minority groups' sociolinguistic background, learning styles, expectations, communication patterns, authority structure, and social organization are at odds with the mainstream culture (P. Portes, 1996b). The argument is that since schools are unable to accommodate these differences, they contribute to the negative experience of minority children, which could explain the subsequent poor academic outcomes of some minority children.

The cultural-ecological theory examines minority education from a macro perspective to understand how political, historical, economic, and social context affect different minority groups (Hayes, 1992). Ogbu (1993) identified two key factors for understanding the academic performance of minority youth in an urban society. The first is the type of cultural difference between the minority group and the majority group; the second is whether the minority group's immigrant status is voluntary (those who came to America freely) or involuntary (those who became Americans through slavery or conquest). Ogbu's cultural ecological theory challenged the cultural deprivation or discontinuity framework that blames the academic underachievement of minority groups on the cultural deficits of the home and various deprivations in home, school, and community (Reis & Diaz, 1999).

According to Ogbu (1987), voluntary immigrants perceive opportunity in the United States and perceive education as the key to advancement, unlike involuntary immigrants who have a long history of exclusion and hence mistrust for what education can offer to them. Involuntary minority groups have academic difficulties due to their response to their forced incorporation and treatment in society. Ogbu (1992) believed that involuntary minority groups develop an oppositional identity, whereby such groups construct their identity in defiance of their subordination by the majority group. This has also been referred to as the blocked opportunities hypothesis and oppositional frame of reference (Kao & Tienda, 1998). The blocked opportunities hypothesis states that some minority groups are motivated to work hard in school due to the perception that education leads to upward mobility, whereas some lack motivation for academic achievement due to the perception that hard work will do little for their future (Kao & Tienda, 1998). In an oppositional frame of reference, involuntary minority groups construct what is valued in their culture in opposition to what is valued in mainstream culture (Ogbu, 2004). For example, devaluing academic achievement because it is associated with mainstream white culture is one way that some minority group members show oppositional behavior.

Ogbu (1993) described the primary cultural difference as the original pre-contact culture of the minority group, whereas the secondary cultural difference is developed in response to treatment of the minority group after contact with the majority group. He concluded that voluntary minority groups such as the participants in this study have higher academic achievement irrespective of their primary cultural differences from the dominant group due to the following reasons. First, voluntary immigrants perceive their immediate obstacles and barriers as temporary and therefore work towards overcoming them. Secondly, the voluntary immigrants' frame of reference lies in their native country where they were worse off than their current situation in the United States. This leads to optimism that fosters a will to succeed among voluntary immigrants. Ogbu's theory is useful in categorizing different minority groups and offers a general framework for the explanations of the variability in the academic achievements of voluntary and involuntary immigrant groups. But it fails to provide an explanation for the inter-and intra-variability of the various immigrant groups. It is also evident that children from similar social backgrounds can exhibit different academic achievement and aspirations (Elliot & Bempechat, 2002). Furthermore, social class, though important, does not predict academic achievement of some groups (Goyette & Xie, 1999).

Conversely, Ainsworth-Darnell and Downy (1998) argued that differences in family and neighborhood characteristics, rather than an oppositional culture, determine school behavior. Although the residential pattern is salient in the academic outcomes of youth, Ainsworth (2002) found that negative effects of poor inner-city neighborhoods on academic outcomes could be mediated through factors such as social capital and control and group collective socialization.

The educational attainment of immigrants is affected by multiple factors including motivation for migration, perceptions of opportunities in the host country, and perceived reward for educational attainment (Ogbu, 1978; Ogbu, 1987; Ogbu & Matute-Bianchi, 1986). The cultural ecological perspective acknowledges the family as the primary agent of achievement socialization and development, but also acknowledges the nature of the interaction between the family and individuals in school adaptation and achievement (Slaughter-Defoe et al., 1990). Although the cultural-ecological theory considers the broader political, social, and economic context in the explanation of minority and immigrant youths' school performance (Trueba, 1991), it fails to recognize the role of "agency" found within some minority groups (Foster, 2004). Agency is used here to describe the ability of the minority group to get things done because of their actions (Bandura, 2001). For example, students from a poor background might be personally motivated to succeed despite the odds and might seek out opportunities that would increase their chance of academic success. Although challenges such as poverty can defeat some people, it can serve as a source of motivation for others.

Immigrant parents with a negative experience due to job discrimination may use the experience to steer their children to excel in academics. For example, Sue & Okazaki (1990) suggested that Asian immigrants emphasize science and math to their children because of the belief that Asians may encounter less discrimination in those fields and due to the perceived objectivity in these fields. Besides, students raised in a family where education is valued will likely derive a sense of educational meaning likely to lead to academic achievement (Bowen & Bowen, 1998). Bowen and Bowen defined such homes in terms of how much emphasis parents place on education through discussions of schoolwork, activities, attendance, and future goals with their children.

Social Cognitive Theory

Portes (1999) noted that agency within a group is a salient factor in the cultural and historical adaptation of various immigrant groups. According to Bandura (2001), agency includes the belief system of a group, the ability to self-regulate, and the various practices through which individuals exercise personal influence. Social cognitive theory offers an agency perspective to human development, adaptation, and change (Bandura, 2001). The agentic perspective of social cognitive theory as applied to this study utilized the constructs of self-efficacy, specifically academic self-concept, and academic self-efficacy. When used in combination with the cultural-ecological theory and social capital theory, they could enrich our understanding of immigrant and minority education such as the case of high-achieving second-generation Nigerian youth.

Students can be empowered with a sense of self-efficacy to draw upon as a coping strategy when faced with problems in their various social contexts. The social cognitive theory recognizes that humans can transcend their situations in life. Families, including immigrant ones when faced with difficulties, might devote material and nonmaterial resources to create a home atmosphere that fosters academic skills, motivation, and orientation (Teachman,1987). Immigrant and minority youth often do not have control over the context under which they live in the United States, but they can be taught self and group enhancing and coping strategies for optimal achievement (Trueba, 1991). How well these youth adapt and succeed in school depends not only on their cognitive ability, individual motivation, and the social and financial resources available to them through their families and communities (Zhou, 1997) but also on how they were socialized to react and respond to their experiences. It is one thing to possess intelligence and motivation, but what happens when young people encounter challenges?

In addition to an attempt to identify what motivates high-achieving second-generation Nigerian youth, one of the goals of this research is to examine how high-achieving second-generation Nigerian youth respond to difficulties in terms of academic and social relations with their peers in school settings. Therefore, it is important to examine the role of self-efficacy beliefs in their academic outcomes. Students with self-efficacy apply cognitive and metacognitive approaches to their understanding of the learning materials when the difficulty of the task on hand increases (Walker, 2003).

In other words, students will increase efforts dispensed and possibly seek help rather than give in when faced with challenges. One might also argue that such students have self-determination and resiliency.

Meece & Kurtz-Costes (2001) stated that despite the daunting economic and social barriers some ethnic minority families face, several resources have enabled numerous ethnic minority children to excel in schools. Such resources can be in the form of cultural beliefs and the ethos of their ethnic groups. It is time that researchers key in on why some minority groups succeed against some odds. The beliefs that students establish and hold to be true about themselves are critical in their success or failure in school (Pajares, 2003). Such beliefs could be rooted in the capital students bring from the home and community, regardless of the other factors such as race that could place youth at a disadvantage.

Social Capital Theory

Social capital (Bourdieu, 1986; Coleman, 1988) is a valuable framework for the study of minority and immigrant students' academic outcomes (Hao & Brunstead-Bruns, 1998; Stanton-Salazar, 1997). Bankston, Caldas, and Zhou (1997) proposed that social capital could accrue from an immigrant group's ethnicity in the relationships found within each immigrant group. Immigrant parents may have ethnic and cultural forms of social capital in the absence of social capital as often conceptualized for middle-class Americans (Bankston, 2004; Zhou & Bankston, 1998; Zhou, 1997). These scholars noted that ethnic communities have unique social capital that needs to be tapped in the research on minority children. But the first step is to identify such capital and where it resides in different groups. I have observed that Nigerians in the United States belong to several WhatsApp chat groups, and they use these forums to share information, announce family news including graduations, deaths, marriages, births, and to solicit funds and support in time of need.

Kao (2004) indicated that social capital could accrue to individuals through obligations between individuals in a group. As immigrants are often isolated from white people, they have less social capital. But immigrants from the same ethnic group could create social capital by sharing information through informal groups. Kao (2004) noted that immigrant groups could share information on how to navigate the educational system in the United States. Nigerian immigrants share information through their ethnic, professional, and religious affiliations. In today's world, technology and social media have made it more efficient to share information between groups and individuals.

Social capital can also reside at school in the form of community ties; include bonds between parents and schools; and reside at home (Parcel & Dufur, 2001). Kao and Rutherford (2007) noted that although researchers have examined how social capital can affect the academic outcomes of youth, few have examined the effects on the children of immigrants. Social capital, like financial and human capital, has the potential to benefit people who have it and could be conceptualized as within the family or outside the family (Kao & Rutherford, 2007). Whereas within family social capital primarily involves interactions between parents and children, outside family social capital includes cultural norms and value systems as well as friendship networks.

Academic achievement is a complex phenomenon, and it is not determined solely by socioeconomic status, race, ethnicity, gender, culture, immigrant status, or any other single variable. Rather, it is a result of the interaction between family, school, and community context, and the characteristics of the child (Okagaki, 2001; Szalacha et al., 2005). As Bandura (1993) noted, one cannot predict students' academic performance based on ability or skills. A combination of factors, including cultural origin, history, the availability of social capital, socio-educational setting together with socioeconomic status, and individual agency influence academic outcomes for second-generation youth (A. Portes, 1999). Since the sociocognitive framework acknowledges that individuals can be proactive and self-regulating as opposed to reactive to environmental and biological forces (Pajares, 2003), this perspective could help shed light on what high-achieving second-generation Nigerians and their parents do to overcome the barriers they face in the schooling of the youth.

As immigrants from an English-speaking nation, Nigerians possess human capital from their educational attainment levels and English language fluency, both deemed assets for immigrants (Portes & Rumbaut, 2001). While social and human capital are important factors in the success of immigrants and their children, Portes and Rumbaut also noted that how well an immigrant group is received and treated in relation to their skin color, plays a vital role in the immigrant groups' outcome.

The academic outcomes of high-achieving second-generation Nigerian youth can be influenced by their family experiences, their personal characteristics and efforts, academic interest, and their ability to network with others. Psychosocial attributes such as academic self-concept can be a salient factor in understanding academic performance with regards to why some students succeed in school while others fail (Corbiere et al., 2006).

CHAPTER 2

Background of Nigerian Immigration and Immigrants in the U.S.

Nigeria is in West Africa and has the largest population of any African country (Omoyibo, 2002). In the years 1980 and 1990, approximately a third of Black immigrants to the United States came from Nigeria (Djamba, 1999). Also, most of the immigrants from Africa in the 1990s came from Nigeria (Lobo, 2001). Nigeria, a former British colony, sends more emigrants to the United States than any other African country (Massey et al., 2007).

Because Nigeria is Africa's largest oil producer, the drop in oil prices in the 1980s created economic hardships that propelled many Nigerians to migrate away, with an estimated 15 million or more residing overseas (Booker & Minter, 2003). From 1990 to 2000, the population of African-born U.S. residents grew from 364,000 to more than 881,000, thus more than doubling in a decade (Grieco, 2004). Based on the United States 2000 Census data, a conservative estimate indicated that between 200,000 and 300,000 Nigerian immigrants and second-generation Nigerians (Booker & Minter, 2003) and approximately 1.7-million sub-Sahara Africans reside in the United States (Roberts, 2005). In 2018, it was estimated that 374,311 Nigerian-born people resided in the United States (Fox, 2020).

Nigerian immigrants are part of the new wave of immigrants coming from developing regions of the world in greater numbers (Rumbaut, 1994b). Like recent immigrants from Asia, Latin America, and Africa, they reflect diversity in terms of class, languages, cultures, migration histories, and ways of incorporation (Rumbaut, 1994a). Black African immigrants, including Nigerians, have the highest educational attainment of any group in the United States (Butcher, 1994; Massey et al., 2007), which is reflected in their migration history because many came to the United States initially to acquire an education (Takougang, 1995). In recent years, Nigerians have emigrated to the United States because of the U.S. Diversity Visa Program, which opened immigration to regions of the world that formerly had been underrepresented in the immigration group (Takyi, 2002). This initiative aimed to attract highly qualified, skilled, and professional immigrants to the United States and led to the high selectivity of the Nigerian immigrant pool (Massey et al., 2007).

African immigrants, including many Nigerians, often arrive in the US with professional, managerial, and technical skills; 44% of African immigrants who declared an occupation fell into those categories compared with 34% of all immigrants (Lobo, 2001). Of the 5000 practicing physicians from Africa residing in the US, more than 79% of them came from South Africa, Nigeria, Ghana, and Ethiopia in that order (Hagopian et al., 2004). The number of African immigrants including Nigerians is undoubtedly likely to continue to increase (Kent, 2007).

Nigerian immigrants, like other African immigrants in the United States, are a self-selected group of skilled and motivated people. They left Nigeria due to the economic and political changes, contributing to a brain drain in Nigeria (Lobo, 2001; Roberts, 2005; Takougang, 1995).

Like other African immigrant populations, Nigerian immigrants are geographically dispersed (Logan & Deane, 2003). Texas, New York, Maryland, California, and Georgia have the largest populations of Nigerian-born residents in the US; combined, they account for more than 50% of the total foreign-born population from Nigeria in the US (Grieco, 2004). The children of Nigerian immigrants are likely to come from two-parent households (Hernandez, 2012).

While some Nigerian immigrants, like other highly educated immigrants from India, Korea, and Japan, live in wealthy districts—affording their children the opportunity to attend good schools (Miller & Tanners, 1995), others might find themselves living in less desirable communities with potential implications for the educational outcomes of their children. A quarter of the African immigrant population is concentrated around the ten largest metropolitan regions in the U.S., but they are likely to live in racially integrated neighborhoods (Massey et al., 2007). Nigerian families residing in urban areas with underfunded schools adopt strategies to ensure that their children obtain a good education. Such families might send their children to parochial or magnet schools, as many parents in the study opted to do for their children. Although Nigerian immigrants have the highest educational attainment level of any other group in the United States, their median household income trails that of the Asians and white Americans, based on the 2003 Census data. However, their median income is higher than the median income of African-Americans and Afro-Caribbean groups (Massey et al., 2007).

Researchers have found that no single factor determines the academic outcomes of second-generation youth. Rather, personal, family, school, and other contextual factors interact with each other to influence the educational outcomes of youth from immigrant backgrounds (Okagaki, 2001; Kim, 2002; Szalacha et al., 2005). Hence Okagaki's (2001) triarchic model of academic achievement, which takes a holistic approach to focus on how school, family, and social identity influence children's achievement, appears to be an appropriate lens through which to examine this group. The experiences of high-achieving second-generation Nigerian youth could be impacted by the way these youth perceive themselves and their academic abilities. Although school and family indicators seem self-explanatory, social identity refers to the way children view themselves within our society in general and within academic settings, which shapes the way children approach and perform in school (Okagaki, 2001). There is increased research on the role of academic self-efficacy as a determinant of a person's academic outcome. According to Sharma and Nasa (2014), individuals with similar backgrounds can have different academic outcomes due to their experiences and how they interpret such experiences, as well as their beliefs and perceptions from the past. The academic outcomes of high-achieving second-generation Nigerian students cannot be attributed to a one-dimensional factor but to various factors (Alomar, 2006).

CHAPTER 3

Profiles of the Youth Participants, Then and Now

As mentioned, the second-generation Nigerian youth in the study had demonstrated academic credentials as evident in their GPA, class rank, standardized test scores, and enrollments in competitive private and Ivy League colleges. Among the college-age participants in the individual in-depth interview, all six attended an Ivy League or a highly selective college. Four were enrolled in an Ivy League college. One participant who graduated from a highly selective college received a graduate degree from an Ivy League college. The sixth youth was enrolled in a selective college. Among the two high school seniors in the sample, one had enrolled in an Ivy League college, and the other had enrolled in a highly selective college.

Each youth participant in the study completed a survey, which asked for biographical, demographic, and family background information, as well as the respondent's opinion about cultural identity. The profiles were generated from the completed surveys, in-depth interviews, and researcher reflexivity notes based on observations. Information about where participants are as of June 2020 was collected from online social media and personal knowledge of some of the participants through their parents.

Interviewee A

Interviewee A was a 15-year-old sophomore in a suburban high school. His older sibling was a high school senior in a magnet urban school in the city where they previously resided. His younger sibling attended a magnet inter-district middle school located in the same urban city they lived in before relocating to their current suburban home. His parents purchased a home three years earlier in an adjacent suburb, and as a result, he started his high school career in this new setting. He lived with both parents and his two siblings. His parents were from the Igbo group in Nigeria and were college graduates with full time employment, one in a healthcare facility and the other in a factory. The interviewee was a very articulate and wise young man who exhibited maturity beyond his age in the way he expressed his views of life. For example, when discussing the issue of peer pressure, he told me that he had concluded that his education was more important than being cool and so devised strategies to deal with peer pressure. He indicated that he was "friends with everyone but claimed nobody as a close friend."

This lanky youth, who identified himself as Nigerian-American, was actively involved in extra-curricular activities at school and the community. He was invited to be a youth representative on the library board in the town he resided in and was the only youth on that board. Consequently, he had been featured in the local newspaper for his community involvement and for being the first youth invited to sit on one of the local boards of his town. His essays were frequently featured in the teen section of the regional daily newspaper. He indicated that he had a passion for writing and would like to pursue a career in journalism. He explained that his parents had tried to guide him to a career in medicine or law because he was a good student and they perceived better job prospects for him in those areas.

He acknowledged that attendance at an inter-district urban magnet elementary school did not fully prepare him for the academic rigors of his current suburban high school. As a result, he had to struggle to catch up during his freshman year. Although his average is in the upper "B" range, he believes that he can always do better. He reported that his GPA was a 3.7 and ranked himself in the top 10% of his class. He appeared to be struggling with the reality that his grades had gone from all As in the urban school he came from to a B average in his new suburban high school.

His address placed him in another high school located in the south end of the town he resided in, but he attended the high school in the north section of town that is perceived to be superior. Minority children in this town received waivers to attend the north end school to racially balance the high schools. All that was needed was for the family to apply for their child to attend the school in the north end. This young man seemed excited about having other second-generation Nigerian youth who are highly visible and in leadership positions in his high school. This was in contrast with his elementary school years in an urban setting where he felt isolated and teased by other kids (He identified the teasers as African- Americans). He expressed admiration for the Nigerian community and how they raised their children. He was optimistic and expressed that regardless of what career path he pursued in the future, he would like to contribute to society.

The youth was interviewed on February 22, 2007 and as of 2020, his goals have changed. He graduated with a BS in public administration, earned two master's degrees, worked for the federal government for a while and is currently enrolled in a third master's degree in international language development at an Ivy League university, hoping to earn a doctorate. Both his parents are college graduates with bachelor's degrees, and it is apparent that this young man has surpassed his parents' educational attainment level. He did not pursue his dream of a career in journalism but neither did he follow his parents' dream of a career as a physician or lawyer. Rather, he carved his niche in an entirely different field and successfully created his path in international language in foreign service with the United States government, an area his parents could not have imagined as a possibility.

Interviewee B

Interviewee B was a 19-year-old junior in a highly selective Ivy League college who was introduced to me by my daughter, who graduated from the same college the previous year. This connection provided access to this student and the other five participants in a focus-group interview at this college. Interviewee B was in a pre-med program, majoring in psychology and neuroscience. She was the oldest of four children and grew up in a suburb in one of the Mid-Atlantic States. She attended a public high school and described the town's demographics as changing from all-white to diverse, due to an influx of immigrants and other minorities. Both of her parents were well educated and employed. Her dad was a physician, and her mother, who had a law degree, was a realtor. Her mother was from the Yoruba group and her father from another major group in southwest Nigeria, but she admitted that she identified more with her Yoruba side because of their greater number in the United States. She identified her ethnicity as Nigerian-American but acknowledged the highly contextualized nature of ethnic identity.

She was a pleasant and respectful young lady and seemed to have some interest in second-generation Blacks and the issue of affirmative action. She generously shared with me a college research paper she had completed on affirmative action and it was apparent that it troubled her that some white people attribute the presence of Black students like herself at elite colleges to affirmative action, discounting the efforts and hard work that led to their admission to such colleges. She also kindly volunteered to help me locate other students for the focus-group interview I conducted on her campus. During the focus-group interview, she mentioned that she had wanted to attend a competitive non-Ivy college in the Midwest, but when the Ivy League school's acceptance letter arrived in the mail, she had no choice but to accept because her parents wanted the Ivy League education for her. She understood that if her parents were paying for college, she was Ivy-bound, no questions asked. This supports the popular notion that Nigerian parents aim for prestigious colleges that bring them status. The focus-group participants echoed the same sentiments.

Interviewee B shared her experiences growing up as the oldest child in an immigrant family, describing herself as a "guinea pig" for her parents. Though her parents were strict with her in her younger years, they later relaxed and allowed her younger siblings more freedom than she ever had. She noted that her parents had become more "Americanized" and have allowed her younger siblings to "Americanize" as well—alluding to more relaxed rules for her siblings. She shared that as the oldest child, she was clearly expected to be a role model for her siblings, and her parents often let her talk to her siblings about school and course selections.

She was unassuming, even though she was a high achiever. She graduated from high school with a GPA of 3.71 (unweighted) and 4.40 (weighted). She scored 1430 out of 1600 on the SAT and ranked herself in the top 10% of her high school graduating senior class. She was a National Merit Finalist, National Achievement Scholar, and a member of the National Honor Society, in addition to other awards and activities. She indicated that she was happy to be recognized on a national test like the National Merit Scholarship program. She expressed concern about being racialized and people looking at her achievements as being attributed to affirmative action rather than to her efforts.

She continued to be involved in extra-curricular activities in college although she admitted that her involvement took time away from her studies. She was extremely committed to civic engagements and wanted to help people, through her future career as a physician. She also admitted that when she was growing up, people around her, including her parents, family friends, and relatives had expected her to be a physician, but she naturally came to like the idea.

The interviewee, who was the first of three siblings in her family to be identified for the gifted and talented program in 3rd grade, skipped the 4th grade. She recalled being teased in elementary school for being too young, and for "talking and dressing white." As a result, she learned to code-switch depending on whom she was around. She acknowledged that code-switching was a way for her to negotiate her multiple environments and identities. Although her parents often expressed concern over her code-switching to African-American vernacular, she argued that identity was highly contextualized and that she could identify herself as an African-American in certain situations. She was concerned that some Nigerian parents have bought into negative media portrayals of African-Americans and, as a result, shield their children from African-Americans. She also shared that her mother and a group of other Nigerian parents, started a Nigerian Parents Association in their school district to help other Nigerians with young children negotiate the school system and expose the younger children to the successful older ones as role models.

Since her interview in April 2007, she has not only earned a bachelor's degree from one of the top Ivy League colleges but also earned MD and MPH degrees from other Ivy League universities and currently works for a federal agency in a leadership capacity, following her dream of public service. She surpassed her dad's MD degree and accomplished her goal.

Interviewee C

Interviewee C was the youngest of three children. She was a 17-year-old high school senior. Her older sister was a law student, and her brother was an undergraduate at a local state university. She attended an urban magnet elementary school before her family moved to a suburb at the onset of her middle school years. She subsequently enrolled in a local public school and later was selected to attend a math-and-science-themed magnet high school in the capital of the New England state they resided in. This was supplemental to the local public high school because of her educational ability in the sciences, as demonstrated from testing. She indicated that attending two schools made her days extremely long. The magnet school was established to attract suburban students into city schools to foster racial integration. She seemed young for her age but appeared to be an extremely bright and independent lady. She lived with both her parents who are ethnic Yoruba, but she identified herself as Nigerian-American. Her mother was an accountant, and her father was an administrator at one of the state hospitals. Her father was also completing his doctoral studies at the time of this interview.

This interviewee's GPA was 3.9 (un-weighted) and she scored 2010 out of a possible 2400 on SAT. She graduated three months after the interview as the valedictorian of her senior class; she rated herself in the top 5% of her class at the time she completed the survey.

She was accepted at an Ivy League university where she intended to study engineering. She aspired to obtain a PhD in the sciences with a career interest in research in the development of alternate fuel sources. Though she appeared young and unassuming, she had lofty goals. She complained about the regimentation of the high school curriculum and her inability to explore her interests in the arts. She admitted that she did not need to work hard to stay at top of her class. She appeared to be unchallenged by her curriculum despite her enrollment in AP classes. She opted to take one elective class as AP as an independent study by doing additional work so that she could maintain her class rank and use the credit for college. She admitted that school was easy for her and that she typically completed her homework during the school day.

Following her interview in May 2007, Interviewee C graduated from an Ivy League university with a bachelor's degree in engineering and works as an engineer. Her father completed his doctorate. While this participant did not reach her educational aspiration of getting a doctorate, she is a successful Ivy League graduate with an engineering degree and career in the engineering field.

Interviewee D

Interviewee D was the oldest participant in the study at 25. She grew up on the West Coast and attended a parochial (Catholic) high school in a suburb and an elite private college on the West Coast. At the time of the interview, she had just completed her MS degree in management at a top New England Ivy League university and had received a job offer from one of the major financial firms on Wall Street. What was interesting about this interviewee was her depth and breadth of knowledge about second-generation Nigerians. I found her while browsing for information on second-generation Nigerians on the web. I came across an article she wrote about second-generation

Igbo youth not learning their culture from their parents, who did not take the time to teach them about it and how she would have loved to be able to speak Igbo. I sent her an e-mail explaining my study with an invitation to participate. Her interview was the longest of the project. It lasted for over three hours, compared to an average of 50 minutes for most of the other participants. She was brilliant, assertive, and extremely articulate.

She was the oldest of four children and grew up with both parents. Her mom was a chemist and her dad a scientist. Both of her parents were Igbo, and she identified herself as Igbo-American. She convinced her parents to send her to a private high school to get a better education. Her parents took second jobs, and she took a part time job to help offset the additional expenses of attending a private school. She described the isolation she faced in the private high school, as most of the kids were from upper middle-class homes and, as a result, she chose to socialize outside school. She used participation in extra-curricular activities as a coping strategy, and as a way of making friends based on common interests.

In college, she met many second-generation African students in her age group for the first time and her world opened. She had to negotiate her identity between bilingual Nigerian students who grew up in Nigeria with Igbo fluency and her group of second-generation Igbo Nigerians who grew up in the United States without knowing how to speak the language. There was the issue of who was the authentic Igbo or Nigerian between the two groups. Even though she identified herself as Igbo-American, she explained that her identification was fluid and contextual depending on the audience. She expressed the importance of networking with African-Americans, especially for professional purposes.

Her high school GPA was 4.4 (weighted), and she scored 1490 out of 1600 on the SAT. The valedictorian of her class, she pointed out that because of the type of high school she attended and due to her independence, her parents did not have to involve themselves heavily in her education, though her mom was now involved in the education of her younger siblings who were attending a public school.

She discovered economics and venture capitalism in college and switched her major from pre-med to economics to her parents' dismay. She subsequently convinced her parents, who both have master's degrees, that it was the best field for her. After college, she consulted for a year before pursuing a graduate degree. Her parents eventually understood that she could make a living in that field after she opened a consulting firm—in preparation for graduate school. After one year, as was the norm for prospective business school applicants, she applied to an Ivy League college for a master's degree in management, and upon graduation, landed her investment banker job on Wall Street.

This youth opined that Igbo people did not have respect for business as a college major, noting that Igbo people's ideas of that field was limited to the import and export business often dominated by uneducated people in Nigeria. As a result, and in a marked contrast with the Yoruba people, Igbo parents discourage their children from majoring in business.

This interviewee spoke to me in May 2007, and since then has reached her goal of becoming an investment banker. She earned degrees from elite and Ivy League colleges and created her path to success in the financial sector—but not in medicine as her parents had wished. She has observed that there are many second-generation Nigerian youth now working in finance, and that this is a new field for Nigerian parents. Second-generation Nigerians such as this youth are pushing beyond career paths and success as defined by their parents to create and define career paths and success of their choice in their terms.

Interviewee E

Interviewee E was a 17-year-old senior in the magnet component of an urban high school. She was extraordinarily articulate and exhibited a tremendous level of confidence during the interview. When asked how she ethnically identified herself, she went beyond the ethnic identification of Nigerian identity and included African-American, and she described her traits as "outspoken, charming, and ambitious." Her leadership skills and other qualities landed her one of the two seats as a student representative at the State School Board of Education in the New England state where she resided.

The youngest of four children, she was an independent, determined, and focused young lady. Her older siblings were college graduates, including two attorneys who began their college careers as pre-med students. During the interview, she described herself as being in the top 10% of her graduating class and shared that she wanted to be a surgeon. Based on her class rank and resumes, she could have attended her state university for little or nothing, but she chose to attend an elite private college in the Mid-Atlantic region. She looks up to her siblings, including one who attended an elite private college, as models of success. Although she indicated that she was self-motivated, she did mention that she derived some motivation from her parents, as well as from her goals.

She lived with her parents whom both had post-graduate degrees. Ranked in the top 1% of her class, she scored 1750 out of 2400 on the SAT and reported her GPA as 3.8. She was actively involved in several extra-curricular activities and appeared to be extremely comfortable in her own skin. She believed that she had a voice in the world and would use her voice to express her opinion on important issues. She liked to walk to the beat of her own drum and indicated that she intended to leave her unique marks in this world. This young lady was lucid and a natural leader and was actively involved in many extra-curricular activities.

I spoke with Interviewee E in June 2007. She subsequently graduated from college and attended medical school outside the country and is now a physician. While both her parents had a master's degree at the time of the interview, this participant exceeded her parents' educational attainment and met her goal of being a physician.

Interviewee F

Interviewee F was a 19-year-old who had just completed her junior year at a competitive private college in New England. She was the youngest of five children who all attended a parochial school up to high school, except for one older sister who chose to attend a magnet public high school close to their house. Her older sisters were college graduates; two completed graduate degrees.

She was third in her high school graduating class and scored 1220 out of 1600 on the SAT. No information was provided about her GPA at the time of her graduation from high school. What was remarkable about this student was her determination to focus on her goal. She knew since elementary school that she wanted to be a clinical psychologist to help people who do not have access to such professionals. Her desire to go into this field came from the counseling she provided to a distressed classmate in elementary school. She was also pursuing a double major in nursing as a backup. She grew up with both parents who are from the Igbo ethnic group. Her mother was a registered nurse (BSN) and her father had a master's degree in engineering. He worked as a high school substitute teacher at the time of the interview. A humble youth in her demeanor, she seemed very sure of what her goals were, as she had a clearly defined career path and a road map with a fallback plan.

Since our conversation in June 2007, this interviewee did not waiver in pursuing her dream of becoming a clinical psychologist and is now a practicing clinical psychologist after earning her doctorate in psychology, surpassing both of her parent's educational attainments while following her passion.

Interviewee G

Interviewee G, also interviewed in June 2007, was the third child in her family and had many siblings. She was an 18-year-old who had just completed her first year in an Ivy League college where her two older siblings are enrolled. There were pure joy and ecstasy around this youth. She and her older siblings attended parochial schools. She was the valedictorian of her senior class like her older sister and scored 1890 out of 2400 on her SAT. She reported her GPA at the end of her high school career as 4.0 and was active in several extra-curricular activities in high school. Because her parents were devout Roman Catholics, the church played a significant role in her upbringing and that of her siblings. She admitted that religion was the center of her life and expressed gratitude to her parents for bringing her up in the church.

She was very candid about her experiences and discussed the challenges of going from an urban parochial high school to a competitive Ivy League college. According to the participant, she had to compete with much better-prepared students who attended elite private schools and well-funded suburban high schools and said she was focused on her goal of being a physician with a determination to work harder despite her under-preparation in high school.

Both of her parents were from the Igbo ethnic group and were college graduates. Her mom was an educator, and her father was a self-employed accountant who had recently suffered a major health setback. Her mother also ran a language/cultural program where she taught the Igbo language and culture to children born to Igbo parents. The program provided her children the opportunity to learn and teach the Igbo language and culture. Interviewee G was actively involved in extra-curricular activities in high school but had curtailed her involvement in college to devote more time to her studies. Yet she believed that there were tremendous benefits in getting involved in activities. She shared that she was being actively recruited to lead some organizations on her Ivy League campus.

Interviewee G graduated from an Ivy League college with two master's degrees and works in a leadership capacity in a hospital. Although she aspired to be a physician, she is successful in the field she ended up in. One would never know how her father's health challenges impacted her ultimate educational attainment as it did to her brother, Interviewee I. Nevertheless, she surpassed her parents' education and career attainment. In addition to two Ivy League degrees, she created her path to success.

Interviewee H

Interviewee H was a 20-year-old and the older sister to Interviewee G. Like her sister, she attended parochial schools and graduated as the valedictorian of her senior class. She graduated with a perfect 4.0 GPA and scored 1320 out of 1600 on the SAT. Because she was the oldest of many children, her parents learned about American schools as they raised her, making her a "guinea pig" like Interviewee B. She was not allowed to socialize outside the home and church in her early years, but her parents "relaxed their strict rules" when she was in high school. Her mother described her as being "another mother" in the home because she was very responsible. She assumed the mantle of leadership for her siblings after her dad suffered a catastrophic health setback and her mother's time was primarily devoted to her father's care.

She was highly intellectual, and she aspired to a career as a researcher in the pharmaceutical field after obtaining a doctorate in engineering. She not only identified her goals and defined them, but also secured all the financing through a scholarship to pay for her education up to the doctoral level. She was energetically involved in several activities in high school and continued to be involved in college. She was the second youth to identify herself as Igbo-American rather than Nigerian-American. Her mother, who was an educator, ran an Igbo language and cultural program and enmeshed her children in the program. Interviewee H and her siblings understand the Igbo language and can speak and read in the language. She indicated that she realized early on that her parents would be unable to pay for her college education. So, she spent hours in her junior year searching for scholarship money. She was also a Jackie Robinson Scholar in addition to all the other awards she received at graduation from high school.

Following her interview at the end of June 2007, Interviewee H earned two degrees from an Ivy League college and worked in a pharmaceutical company for many years before resigning her position to pursue a corporate MBA from a top mid-western college. She now works for a top international consulting firm. This participant had aspired to a career as a researcher in the pharmaceutical industry after a doctorate. However, she switched her goals after working in the pharmaceutical industry for many years. There is no way to determine how or if her father's illness and her experiences working in a pharmaceutical company impacted her goals and educational attainment. However, she took a major risk by resigning her corporate secure job to pursue another avenue where she could create her unique path to success, defying how her parents and other Nigerian parents guide their children to certain careers for job security amongst other reasons. Her career interest in research has changed to management in the consulting sector, and one wonders how her experiences in the pharmaceutical industry influenced her decision to switch careers. Both her parents earned master's degrees, but she added an executive MBA to her two Ivy League degrees.

Interviewee I

Interviewee I was the brother to both Interviewees G and H. He attended the same parochial high school as his siblings. He was 19 years old and had just completed his sophomore year in the same Ivy League college that both his sisters attended. He was the first college-age male in my in-depth interview group, and I was thrilled about his participation in the study. There was a lot of optimism in the air as he talked about his experiences and future. He had a lot to share and could barely contain his exuberance for life and his goals.

He bared his soul as he described the academic difficulties in his first year in college that humbled him. In his words, he was "ill-prepared" for the rigor of an Ivy League school in the urban parochial high school he graduated from, he lacked good study habits and admitted to being a social butterfly. Also, after his dad suffered a major health setback, Interviewee I, as the oldest son, returned home to help with his father's care. His dad later passed on.

These experiences and challenges made him to take a good look at his future and to re-examine his college major. Initially, he was enrolled in a pre-med program. After a disappointing academic performance, he explored other majors and started contemplating majoring in business, public policy, and sociology with the goal of attending law school. He identified himself as Nigerian-American and had a circle of second-generation Nigerians he called his core friends.

He related to me that the hardest thing he ever had to do was to face his parents and to inform them of his decision to change his major. As the oldest son, his parents had certain expectations of him, as Nigerian parents often do for the oldest son and oldest daughter. This includes the expectation that older children will serve as role models for their younger siblings. Growing up, these expectations were reinforced by his parents, and other family members, reminding him that he could not lower the bar as the first son. He knew he did not want to disappoint his parents.

He was surprised, then, that his parents did not express disappointment over his major change. His mother acknowledged during an interview with her that they set extremely high expectations for their children so that if they fall short, they can still land on something. This youth's resiliency and ability to bounce back from challenges was remarkable. He was deeply spiritual and had a wealth of friends. He was easily drawn to people.

Growing up, he was motivated by his parents as well as his siblings. He mentioned that there was sibling competition between his siblings. He said there was a time when he resented his older sibling, who always overshadowed him in academic performance. But as they grew older, they motivated each other. He felt he could have done better in high school if he had studied harder. He had not needed to study hard and performed well with minimum effort. He graduated as number seven in his senior year class with a GPA of 3.6 and scored 1340 out of 1600 on the SAT. In college, he had a rude awakening as he lacked good study skills, which he said were never taught in his high school. As a result, he struggled academically and had to learn how to study to overcome his academic difficulties.

This young man clearly had a future in the public sector area. He was vocal, articulate, involved, well-informed, and social. He finally found his niche in the social sciences. He acknowledged that he was now happy with what he was studying in college after he changed his major and the satisfaction was reflected in his current grades. His excitement about life and the future were visible and palpable as he spoke.

Like his older sister, he grew up involved in his mother's Igbo language and cultural program. He discussed at length the value of second-generation Nigerians being able to identify with their roots because it allowed them to be able to relate to their peers of the same background while strengthening their identity to relate to the outside world. According to this youth, those second-generation Nigerians who were not taught the Nigerian culture lacked the skills to "code-switch" into Nigerian cultural patterns in the presence of their peers and often avoided their peers from the same background. His observation was that such youth "stopped being Nigerians as it was too hard for them." He appeared to relish the ability to slip into multiple cultures and joked about how the second-generation Nigerian youth mimicked their Nigerian parents in skits during cultural awareness week on campus for entertainment.

Interviewee I was interviewed in July 2007. He withdrew from the Ivy League university during his father's illness and returned home where he graduated from a local university. He earned a master's degree and is pursuing a career in the public sector in a leadership capacity. One thing that stood out about this young man was his optimism during my interview and his resiliency in being able to overcome challenges. He never wavered in his ability to push ahead. Both his parents earned masters' degrees and this participant did not do less for now. I would not be surprised to see him aim for a law degree or a doctorate in the future. For now, he has found success following his true passion in the social sciences and working in the public sector.

Interviewee J

Interviewee J was a 16-year-old senior in a magnet component of an urban high school. She was born in the United Kingdom and came to the United States with her parents at the age of five. They lived in the tri-state area before moving to a New England state where her parents purchased a home. She was the oldest of four children and she was getting ready to apply to colleges when I interviewed her. Her GPA was 3.6 and she was ranked in the top 5% of her class. She scored 1760 out of 2400 on her SAT. Interviewee J aspired to a career in pharmacy.

Her father was a college professor. Her mother, who received a degree in business from the United Kingdom, was home with her younger children while pursuing a master's degree. Interviewee J was involved in extra-curricular activities and volunteered in a day care center in the city where they resided. She was very modest in her appearance and in the way she described her life, yet she was keenly focused on her future and goals.

Both her parents were from the Yoruba ethnic group and she identified herself as Nigerian of Yoruba descent. Her mother indicated that after they moved from the United Kingdom to the United States, Interviewee J was confused about her identity. She wondered whether she was British, Nigerian, or American. Her parents reassured her that she was Nigerian because her parents were from Nigeria.

Interviewee J was interviewed in September 2007. She graduated with a degree in pharmacy and is currently a pharmacist, in a management position. She followed her dream and met her goal. Her father had a doctorate and her mother who held a bachelor's degree at the time of the interview has since completed a master's degree.

Interviewee K

Interviewee K is the 14-year-old brother of Interviewee J and was a sophomore in another magnet urban high school in the city where they resided. They were interviewed on the same day in September 2007, but separately. He originally attended the same magnet high school his sister was enrolled in. Upon discovering that another magnet school in the city was geared towards students interested in the health-related fields, he convinced his parents to allow him to transfer even though the location of that school was less desirable than the magnet school he was attending. His parents checked out his findings and allowed him to transfer. The family was new to the area they lived in, but that did not deter Interviewee K. He kept his eyes open for opportunities that would help him with his future goal. Being new to the city and young was not an obstacle for him.

Interviewee K was an ambitious youth who was dedicated to his education. This 14-year-old student not only knew he wanted to be a physician, but also knew how to get there and was already strategizing on how to achieve his goals. He sought out different extra-curricular activities that would enhance his college and career prospects and identified some extra-curricular activities that would help him to achieve his goal. One of the groups he belonged to had taken him to visit colleges. His Saturdays were devoted to extra-curricular activities. He reported his GPA as 3.4 and rated himself in the top 10% of his class. He had also participated in after-school college preparation programs that help minority youth prepare for and succeed in college. Interviewee K was self-motivated and was diligently working hard towards his goals. His mother expressed surprise that he would like to be a physician, as she does not believe in pushing kids into any profession. Like his sister, he described himself as a Nigerian of Yoruba descent. He was also born in the United Kingdom and came to the United States at the age of 4, and was also confused about whether he was British, Nigerian, or American.

Interviewee K graduated from one of the top Historically Black Universities with a bachelor's and a master's degree and went on to earn a second master's degree in management from an elite university. He works for a sports team. Although he did not pursue his initial goal of becoming a physician, he found success by carving out his own niche while trailblazing in an area that Nigerians do not typically aspire to.

Focus Group Participants

This section discusses the focus-group Ivy League college participants at the time of the interview and thirteen years later. As mentioned earlier, there were six participants in the focus-group interview. One of them also participated in the in-depth interview.

Focus Group Participant 1.

This participant grew up in a suburb and graduated from a public high school. He graduated in the top 10% of his class with a grade point average of 3.6 (unweighted) and had an SAT score of 1350 out of 1600. He was majoring in engineering and aspired to get a master's degree. Both his parents are professors with doctoral degrees. Upon graduation with an engineering degree, he pursued a master's degree and currently works in the corporate sector as an operations manager. Although he did not match his parent's educational attainment, he met his goals, and with a degree from one of the top Ivy League schools and a corporate managerial job, he is deemed successful in his chosen path.

Focus Group Participant 2.

This participant grew up in an urban town and attended a parochial high school. He graduated high school as the school's salutatorian with a weighted grade point average of 4.00 and scored 1300 out of 1600 on the SAT. He was recruited by the college as a student-athlete. Both his parents are professors with doctoral degrees. After graduating with a degree in international and public policy, he earned a JD degree and is a General Counsel. He shared that he was unsure of what to study in college and his father suggested pre-med but after taking a few courses, he realized that medicine was not a good fit for him. His white American mother was more flexible with his options and college major. Like the previous youth, he did not reach his parent's educational attainment levels, but he met his goal of earning a law degree from an elite university and becoming a corporate attorney.

Focus Group Participant 3.

This participant grew up in an urban town and attended a public high school graduating with a grade point average of 5.00, weighted. She did not provide her high school class rank on the survey she completed. She was in a pre-med track and upon graduation, she earned a medical degree and an MFA degree in-between medical school. Her mother is a pharmacist and her father is a physician with combined MD/ Ph. D degrees. This participant followed her MD with an MFA degree and met her career aspiration of becoming a physician; it appears that she also has an interest in literary work.

Focus Group Participant 4.

This participant grew up in a suburban town and graduated from a public high school in the top 10% of her class with a weighted grade point average of 3.8 and an SAT score of 1310 out of 1600. Her father has a master's degree, and her mother has a BS in nursing. She was in a pre-med track and aspired to a career in medicine. I was unable to locate information about this participant to determine her educational attainment to date or her career path upon graduation.

Focus Group Participant 5.

This participant grew up in a suburban town and graduated from a public high school in the top 5% of her class with a weighted grade point average of 3.8 and an SAT score of 1310 out of 1600.

Her father is a college professor with a doctorate and her mother has a bachelor's degree.

I could not locate any evidence that she earned a graduate degree. The participant works for one of the top social media outfits in a management position.

Focus Group Participant 6.

This participant was Interviewee B in the in-depth interview and was the only one who participated in both the in-depth and focus-group interviews. I gained access to the focus-group participants with her help. She lived in a suburban town and graduated from a public high school in the top 5% of her class with a grade point average of 4.4 (weighted) and an SAT of 1430 out of 1600. Her father is a physician and her mother who has a law degree is a realtor. Upon graduation, this participant earned an MD and MPH from other Ivy League colleges and is now a physician as stated earlier. She met her goals regarding educational attainment and career goals.

The academic achievements of second-generation Nigerian youth in this study are aligned to their parents' educational attainment levels, which national data shows have the highest level of education in the United States. Looking at where the participants are today, based on their academic and professional careers, they lived up to the high-achieving definition label. They might not have followed their parents' career plans for them or earned as many degrees, but they found success in their own way—according to their redefined context. Amongst those who participated in the in-depth interviews, all except two who earned professional degrees as an engineer and a pharmacist went on to earn graduate and or professional degrees in pursuit of their career goals or personal interests. In the focus-group participants that I was able to track, all pursued graduate degrees except for the two that I was unable to verify their educational attainments.

According to the study participants, Nigerian parents favor high-status and high-earning careers such as law, medicine, and engineering for their children, which can create conflict between some parents and their children. Such fields not only bring social status to the family but increases the odds of gainful employment and shields the youth from job discrimination because of the technical expertise required in such fields. Nigerian kids often poke fun at how their parents react to certain majors ("What are you going to do with it?"), knowing their parents love pedigrees. The focus-group alluded to the fact that their parents love to brag to friends about their children's careers and elite colleges where their children were admitted. In the words of one of the interviewees, "...Everyone is going to be a doctor, engineer, or lawyer because these are the professions that are worth more and you are always going to have a job." On the contrary, many of the focus-group participants shared that they did not always publicize the fact they were attending an Ivy League college because people looked at them differently. It is possible that the one participant in the focus-group that pursued a graduate degree in fine arts (creative writing) in-between earning a medical degree was pursuing her passion and at the same time meeting her parent's expectations regarding certain careers preferred by Nigerian parents. Many Nigerian parents plead with their children with interest in the arts to first pursue an education in a field where they can secure employment upon graduation before following their passion. One parent in the study encouraged her child to double-major in her passion and nursing. As an example, if a child wants to be a writer, actor, or musician, she or he is encouraged to first earn a medical or engineering degree before pursuing writing, acting, or music career.

Of the sixteen participants interviewed individually, and in the focus-group, nine of them aspired to a career as a physician. In the end, three earned medical degrees and became physicians, three earned engineering degrees, two earned law degrees, one was a pharmacist, one was a clinical psychologist (PhD), one was an investment banker, and five pursued other interests and yet they are all successful in their chosen paths. The high number of participants who aspired to a career in medicine confirms what one participant shared that a friend told her that "all Nigerians are pre-med by default" and confirmed the students' perception that Nigerian parents steer their children to certain careers, especially in medicine. Among the six focus-group participants, four achieved their career goals as physicians, an engineer and as an attorney.

All participants had high academic aspirations and educational attainment goals as evidenced by the interviews. Such goals were influenced by their parents, siblings, relatives, and personal drives. Most of the participants achieved the career goals they set for themselves. Those who deviated created their own paths to success and became trail-blazers in areas their parents might never have thought of as a possibility for their children, such as leadership roles in entirely different fields. These participants followed their hearts, signaling that anything is possible when you pursue your passion. Nigerian parents inculcated in their children the value of education and hard work; with luck, their children will exceed their imaginations. Whether these youth met or exceeded their parents' educational attainment is not as important as whether they have followed their individual definition of success in areas they feel passionate about.

If there is one lesson here, it is that after giving their children a solid educational foundation and after equipping them with the tools to succeed, Nigerian parents should allow their children the room to follow and create their paths. The youth have opportunities that their immigrant parents could not have dreamt of and they are not inhibited by speaking with an accent. Nigerian parents may not have imagined some of the jobs available to their American-born children because their world views growing up in Nigeria are far removed from the twenty-first-century world where their children are growing up. As a result, success may not look exactly like what the parents are familiar with or envision. For example, some of the participants defined success as "being happy" in whatever they chose to do with their careers. Not surprisingly, five participants changed career goals and pursued other interests, and it may not be over yet as some might still change careers in the future as they explore new opportunities or new interests and passion. Nigerian-American parents could not have conceived of their children making a good living working for companies like Google, Facebook, Amazon, and other social media and technology companies a few years ago. Yet these are possibilities for second-generation Nigerian children who are highly educated. Second-generation Nigerians are also gaining inroads into professional sports, entertainment, and media, as with their academic prowess. Often when one sibling cracks a door open, siblings and sometimes cousins will see what is possible and follow— whether in school or sports. Many of the youth in the study followed their older siblings to Ivy League and elite colleges. Parents also use the children of other Nigerians to motivate their children to see what is possible. If someone can do well, why not their children? If one sibling can do it, why not the next sibling? Sometimes, the children compete amongst themselves and emulate their siblings. In sports, you might see siblings following the footsteps of older siblings —like the Ogwumike sisters in Texas where the four sisters are Division 1 basketball players, including WNBA MVP, two who aspire to be doctors, and one, a broadcaster (Fader, 2017). The oldest sister found success through playing basketball in high school and for Stanford University and her three sisters are following in her footsteps. Their parents have found that playing basketball in America brings fame and money and it is working for the family. Playing basketball would not have been an option for the girls and their parents if they resided in Nigeria. I have no doubt that more Nigerians in the United States and beyond will use the Ogwumike Family as a template and model of another avenue to success in America. However, they are likely to still hold their children accountable to do well in school just like the Ogwumike girls. Their story speaks to the power of seeing what is possible and having someone to look up to.

CHAPTER 4

Personal Characteristics of the Youth in the study

History of Academic Achievement

The second-generation Nigerian youth in this study had demonstrated academic credentials through their GPA, class rank, standardized test scores, and enrollments in competitive colleges in the United States of America. This supports a study by Massey et al. (2007), which found that second-generation Black students from Africa, especially from Nigeria, were overrepresented in America's most selective colleges. Such over-representation was greatest in the Ivy League colleges, as was the case in this sample. Among the college-age participants in the individual in-depth interview, all six of them attended an Ivy League or a highly selective college. Four were enrolled in an Ivy League college. Another one who graduated from a highly selective college received a graduate degree from an Ivy League college. The sixth youth was enrolled in a highly selective college. Among the two high school seniors in the sample, one has enrolled in an Ivy League college, and the other has enrolled in a highly selective college.

Another finding that was supported by Massey et al. (2007) was the high selectivity of African immigrants. The parents of high-achieving second-generation Nigerians in this study were college graduates, many of whom hold a professional and master's degrees. It is important to note that selection of youth for the study did not consider the educational background of their parents. To many Nigerian parents, not attending college was not an option and a bachelor's degree was not acceptable. Nigerian parents have transferred these educational aspirations to their children. None of the youth participants, in the individual in-depth and the focus-study group, indicated that a BA was a terminal degree. They aspired to careers that would require a professional or graduate school. One focus-group participant recalled hearing from his father that "BA" stood for "Begin Again" to drive home the need for graduate school. "Begin Again" is an expression that Nigerian parents use to encourage Nigerian youth to pursue graduate education or a professional degree. Parents believe that the more education their children acquire, the more secure their future. Education was so valued in the Nigerian community that participants in the focus-group interview shared that they realized early on that they could get away from house chores and other family obligations with the excuse that they needed to study for a test.

Academic Expectations

All youth who participated in the study had similar experiences when it came to their parents' expectations that they excel in school by doing their absolute best. Nigerian parents expect their children to do well in school and make sacrifices to ensure the academic success of their children. The focus-group referred to it as the "Nigerian thing." To the parents, there was no excuse or room for academic failure, and second-generation Nigerian youth responded with hard work. However, the multiple contexts of their experiences define how they perceive themselves about academic expectations and academic success.

High-achieving second-generation Nigerian youth in the study had high but realistic academic expectations for themselves. Although the youth demonstrated academic achievement as evidenced from their credentials, many were not content with grades less than an A. It appeared that obtaining good grades was important to the youth and that they were used to getting a grade of As in all their classes through high school and expected themselves to continue with As in college. However, they realistically tailored their expectations to meet their goals in different contexts and experiences. Conversely, their expectations were modified according to their experiences and age or as they progressed in their academic and career pursuits. For example, when the college-age youth realized that they could no longer obtain an A in all their classes, they adjusted their expectation by changing their definition of academic success, redefined what constitutes a successful career path, and increased their efforts.

The high school youth who received a grade less than an A felt that their grades could be better, but they also realized that the most important thing was to put in their best effort. This was reflected in the youths' responses to the meaning of academic success. Whereas some youth defined academic success in terms of grades, others broadened the definition to include efforts, persistence, working hard toward their goals, and in the context of academic self-efficacy.

To the question, "What does academic success mean to you?" one participant, a high school senior and a future valedictorian of her senior class indicated that the definition of academic success varied according to individuals. She defined the construct as follows: "For me, it is getting A, but I know for others it is trying as hard as they could even if they don't do well, but I never had that problem." This youth noted during the interview that her suburban high school did not challenge her even with the supplemental education she received from a competitive science-and-math-themed regional magnet school.

Another participant, a high school sophomore responded, "academic success means trying my best and succeeding. Putting my best effort into it is what counts. If I get a B+ in science by putting my best effort, it means more to me that getting an easy A in English because I am really good in English." Another high school sophomore reaffirmed and concurred with this response, "academic success is not really getting an A but doing good, working hard in your studies. This is because not everyone gets straight-As. They do good in some subjects and not in others. Getting straight-As is not everything."

A high school senior responding to the same question said, "academic success is not getting an A in a class but trying your best and you feel that you learned. Sometimes you get an A in a class, but you learned nothing from it. All you did is do your homework and the teacher gave you an A. In other classes you work hard and learn something that will help you in the future and you will not get an A."

Another high schooler included social development in her definition of academic success. A high school senior defined academic success this way: "Success doesn't necessarily mean grades and graduating. Of course, you go through elementary, middle, and high school. You want to leave your mark. You want people to know that you lived. It is not just getting A but proving to yourself that you can prosper as a person. Success is not just academic but social development. It means that you are bettering yourself socially, academically and you are applying the concept learned in everyday life. It is not [just] learning but applying what you learned."

The contextualized nature of the meaning of academic success was reflected in the responses of some of the college-age youth. One participant, a college junior at a highly competitive Ivy League college, defined academic success as "performing well enough in your school classes to be happy with yourself, and also to allow you to achieve your next goal, whatever that might be—graduation from college, being accepted into a graduate school or professional school." Another college student attending an Ivy League college and who survived a challenging academic year defined academic success as, "To me, especially at an Ivy League, I really think it is just graduating. The first step, high school is not good enough. You cannot get far with just a high school diploma. You need at least a bachelor's degree and right now you probably need more than a bachelor's degree. Ten years from now, nobody is going to care about what position (class rank) you were, they will [care] about whether you got the degree." He thrived academically after he changed his major from pre-med to the social sciences and improved his study skills.

The lone graduate student in the sample defined academic success in a multifaceted approach as follows: "For me, academic success has gone through many phases. From K-12, it was about getting into college, scoring well on the standardized tests because the system is score-oriented. For college, it was getting the tools I need for a job and positioning myself for the right type of job. In graduate school, it was about acquiring the knowledge and skills needed to be successful on the job. From a socio-cultural point of view, making my parents proud; being distinguished."

Youth were asked to respond to the question: "How are you doing in school?" This was an attempt to understand how they perceived their academic achievement in relation to their prior history and current context. A participant who was a junior in an Ivy League college with a 1450 out of 1600 on the old SAT, responded to the question as follows: "I guess I am doing fine. I am an average Ivy League student. I did well in high school. College has been a humbling experience. I am a B+ student. I was hoping for a continuation, and that didn't quite happen with my expectation." Many Ivy League students would have been content with a B+ average. But for this youth, B+ average is just "average" alluding to her high academic expectations.

This youth was also involved in several college extra-curricular activities because she felt that college was the place to become involved and extend her social network. College success is more than getting all As but making connections and exploring life and interests. She believed that college was the place to enjoy her life and getting involved made her happy. She appeared to realize that there were other ways to be successful besides getting As in her classes and she had embraced extra-curricular activities as another way to be successful in life.

Another Ivy college youth, who was also the valedictorian of her class, responded to the question, "How are you doing in school?" with "I think I am doing okay. I started out rough because it is an Ivy League college, everything is just harder, and I found out the hard way. So, I think I am doing average." When asked to define average, she hesitantly revealed that her GPA was a 3.00 and to which she added, "I have never done average in school. I have always done better than I did here. Average to me is not what I think I should be. I did better my second semester." She also noted, "I attend an Ivy League college and everyone else here had done above average in high school. If you are above average here, you are exceptional because everyone is above average." She has come to terms with attending an Ivy League school that attracts the best students and she is holding her own given that she graduated from an urban parochial high school that did not adequately prepare her for an Ivy League rigor.

Another Ivy League youth shared the same beliefs when she stated, "all of us here are from the top 10% of our high school classes, and of course we can't all be in the top 10% again. There must be a redistribution of class position. Some of the courses are tough. However, I am holding on my own. I am pre-med with a concentration in neuroscience in the department of psychology."

Youths' Self-Perception

Parents, teachers, and peers play a critical role in shaping how youth perceive their academic abilities (Cole, 1991; Parsons et al., 1982). Researchers have determined that parents' attitudes and beliefs about their children play a vital role in children's self-perceptions of their abilities (Eccles, 1983; Jacobs & Eccles, 1992; Wagner & Phillips, 1992). Agency is a useful concept that can explain how second-generation Nigerian youth develop an academic self-concept growing up. Bandura (2001) defined agency to include an individual's belief system, ability to self-regulate, and ability to exercise personal influence over ones' life. The Nigerian parents in this study empowered their children with a sense of agency. Parents had high academic expectations and taught their children self-regulation and autonomy. At an early age, parents created structure for their children. To Nigerian parents, there was no such thing as "can't do" and no excuses were allowed for academic failure if one has the ability and their children internalized the parental beliefs.

Therefore, high-achieving second-generation Nigerian youth internalized these beliefs of agency from their parents and their community. Youth exhibited agency traits in some of their behaviors. They influenced their parents to send them to the schools that would support their goals. Ukpokodu (2017) noted that teachers of second-generation children do not take time to communicate important information to parents for reasons such as accent of parents resulting in denial of access to opportunities to gifted and talented education for the children. Refusing to accept no for an answer, the second-generation youth in my study challenged guidance counselors to help them find information they needed to meet their goals during college admission process. When their assigned counselors provided minimum help, they sought out other counselors who could help them when their assigned ones were unable to deliver. The youth were proactive in creating favorable relationships with new counselors in anticipation of college recommendations. When asked about how much control they had over their academic success, all youth participants attributed their success to their motivation and partly to their parents and good teachers. This was an indication that they had personal agency. They used such agency to find ways to navigate their academic experiences.

It appeared that the youths' agency originated in their Nigerian ethnic identity, which they credited for their academic success. All youth claimed a Nigerian affiliated identity and believed that Nigerians were successful in academics. Such group identity could be salient in how high-achieving second-generation Nigerian youth perceived themselves as academic achievers. This finding supported the findings of Oyserman et al. (2001), which found that the perception of being in-group as academic achievers could motivate youth and foster academic efficacy. Oyserman et al. (2001) posited that ethnic identity could offer positive protection against low academic efficacy because efficacy was a motivational factor and because belonging to a minority group could have negative consequences, such as stigmatization. Nigerian parents do not give room for their children to be stigmatized so they invest resources to prepare their children for academic excellence. They empower their children with the belief that they can achieve as much as any other child, if not more. The children joke about being asked what happened to the other 5% when they brought home a grade of 95% on a test.

High-achieving second-generation Nigerian youth grew up with educated parents and were exposed to educated Nigerians. Consequently, they had come to view academic achievement as an in-group marker for Nigerians—something valued and expected in their community. They received accolades from family, extended family, and the Nigerian community when they did well in school. The youth also grew up believing in their capability to do well in school. The lone graduate student had indicated that Nigerians, whether in the United States or Nigeria, were "not afraid to tackle any subject." According to her, Nigerians did not feel inhibited and did not grow up with the mentality that somebody could be in their way to success. They had the self-efficacy that said, "I can do it." She felt that such beliefs had been transmitted to high-achieving second-generation Nigerian youth.

All youth in the study indicated that their parents instilled the value of education in them early on. It appeared that these youth had internalized the belief that education was the key to the future. High-achieving second-generation youth did not exhibit an oppositional identity (Ogbu, 1978, 1991) against academic achievement or mainstream society. They did not exhibit any animosity toward the mainstream society or view race as an obstacle to their academic success. These youth exhibited an awareness of race in our society but chose not to dwell on it, focusing on their goals instead. This supports

Ogbu's view that children of voluntary immigrants do not develop an oppositional identity to education.

Motivation

High-achieving second-generation Nigerian youth in this study were motivated to achieve academically and their motivation was attributed to internal and external factors. Many of the youth expressed the need to meet their goals and the need to help others through their career choices as the source of their motivation. Their motivation appeared mostly internal, but parents laid the foundation for the development of that internal drive. Although they credited their parents, family, and Nigerian community as part of their motivation, making their parents happy did not appear directly to be a key motivation for most of them, though it could be at the back of their minds. The youth spoke of how happy their parents were with older siblings and other Nigerian youth who did well in school. They witnessed their parents brag about their accomplished siblings.

When asked what motivated them to do well in school, one Ivy League college participant stated, "My ultimate motivation and goal is to become a physician and a good one. I want to help others and I can do that through medicine, which is the most fundamental way of helping any human being. So, my motivation is to help others." She also credited her family and her family friends as the source of her motivation. She stated, "My motivation comes from my family and their strong emphasis on education." She also indicated that family friends motivated her through their high expectations of her as the oldest child of her parents. As a kid, this participant often heard expressions such as "oh, you are going to be a doctor like your dad?" As she grew up, she realized that she "really" liked medicine and wanted to be a doctor.

The youngest participant, a high school youth, also indicated that he was interested in medicine and was motivated by the desire to help others. However, he also mentioned that he wanted to be a medical doctor because he was good in math and science. He responded to the motivation question with, "I want to be a medical doctor because I like math and science and I want to help others." His choice was based on his perceived academic self-efficacy in math and science. For another high schooler, it was her career interest that motivated her. She stated that she was motivated by her goal of researching alternate energy fuels to find other sources of fuel. She later earned a degree in engineering.

For one high school youth who was a senior, she indicated that she was "motivated by her goals, the end, for the long-term effects of education, for what it gets you in life. Learning teaches you things." Her view was affirmed by another youth with the following statement: "Just knowing that education is the key. I want to go into the pharmaceutical sciences. Without an education, I cannot get there. Doing well in school is the key to succeeding and that's what motivates me."

One college youth at an Ivy League university added that the academic environment she was in was partly her motivation to succeed. She stated, "being in a competitive college setting and my large dreams and goals motivated me to work hard and I can't get there without working hard."

For this college youth attending a competitive college in New England, it was her goals as well as the fear of failure that motivated her to work hard. She knew from grade school that she wanted to be a clinical psychologist and planned to double major in psychology and nursing as a backup to ensure that she would always have a job. She was determined to succeed by choosing a double major to make sure that she had a backup in her career options possibly to, in her words, "avoid failure."

The lone graduate student participant stated, "I am goal-oriented, ambitious, and I have a personality growing up that was bound for success, and I was also motivated by the idea of giving back to the community." Like other participants stated, she said that in addition to her goals, "another important motivation is my parents." She worked hard to convince her parents that she could succeed as an investment banker and she was determined to do so.

One participant talked about the satisfaction of getting good grades as one of his sources of motivation. He stated, "when you get the paper with a 100 on it, you smiled because you did well." He also added negative consequences as a motivation for doing well in school. He noted, "primarily knowing that if I came home with poor grades, it would be the end of my life." When asked to clarity what he meant, he said, "It was the scolding and the complete failure you felt." This sentiment was not shared by his siblings or any other participant in the study.

For this participant, sibling competition was also initially part of his motivation to do well in school, especially having an older sister who performed exceptionally well in school. He described how his siblings motivated him as follows: "Here at my house, it was also a competition with no prize. But at this level, we just do it for ourselves and we are not competing. Out of all of us, it is the oldest three children in the household who are in college and close in age because we have always been in school together and feel that you must be as good. My oldest sister has always motivated me. Part of my motivation to work hard was my sister. She always overshadowed me. At one point, I was bitter towards her for that because I did not get straight-As. I got As and Bs. I was always involved [extra-curricular activities]. My parents always said that the limelight was on my older sister and me because we had to show good examples to the younger ones. For the younger ones, it is easy because they see us."

When asked "What motivated you to work hard in school?" another youth responded, "First my parents. They are always trying to make me get involved and because they [instilled] in me at a young age to do my homework and to study. Now I can do it myself. It is a combination of my environment, my cousins, my extended cousins, and the Nigerian community. A lot of them are lawyers, doctors, married and successful. I do not want to compete or outshine them; I just want to be successful for me. My classmates also help me to do my best."

This participant's experiences also confirmed what other participants said. She stated, "Seeing my sisters and how they succeeded helped to keep me motivated. Also, everyone around me including relatives and parents are sources of motivation." Similarly, focus-group participants indicated that parents used older siblings to motivate the younger ones.

Career Aspirations

Another personal characteristic evident in the finding was that all youth participants had high career aspirations. Such aspiration often required professional training or graduate school, and some youth were motivated by career aspirations, due to a need to give back to the community as previously noted. Youth indicated career interests in medicine, engineering, pharmacy, psychology, and journalism. Three of them indicated they would pursue a doctoral education as terminal degrees.

Among the eleven participants in the in-depth interview group, eight youth indicated that math with a combination of another subject such as English was their strength. Seven youth planned for a career in the health and physical sciences. One youth, who indicated that his strength was in the social sciences, had switched his major from pre-med to business and sociology. Another youth, who planned a career in journalism, indicated that English and geometry were his favorite subjects. The youth in high school were as likely to aspire to careers in the health and physical science as the college youth. Females as well as males were likely to aspire to careers in those same areas. Of the three males in the sample, one aspired to a career in medicine, and two planned to study journalism, business, and sociology. During the in-depth interview, two of the three males indicated that they aspired toward a law degree.

High career aspiration was also found among the focus-group participants. Three of the focus-group participants were in pre-med programs, one in engineering, with the other two majoring in other areas after having considered pre-med. One participant attributed such career aspiration and educational aspiration to having Nigerian parents. He stated, "It is a testament to our upbringing. It is not just at this college but also other colleges. There is a certain approach to education that is taught to the children regardless of the household they grew up in. They are taught that education is first..."

Such parental influence on career paths steered some second-generation Nigerian youth into pre-med programs in college, which also resulted in high attrition rates in pre-med track college majors. As one participant attending an Ivy League college observed in his college campus, "Of my closest friends of five, three started in pre-med, two are still there. But of all my Nigerian friends in general, 50%

started as pre-med and now you can easily cut that into half. Everyone discovers that you cannot force yourself into it. If you do not have it within you, you cannot do it. Even with engineering, I know people who after three years in the program changed their major. If you force yourself into it, it is not going to be your favorite."

Some youth aspired to careers in fields where a parent was employed. One participant who grew up hearing "Oh, you're going to be a doctor like your dad" is interested in pursuing medicine as a career goal. On the other hand, some Nigerian parents want different career directions for their children. When one of the focus-group participants informed his engineer father that he wanted to study engineering, his father's response was, "Oh, are you sure you don't want to be a doctor?" According to this youth, engineering was no longer good enough for his dad even though it is a field desired by many Nigerians for their children. This implies that there is a pecking order for the high-status fields that Nigerian parents desire for their children.

Such observations indicated that parents steered youth into certain careers for various reasons. One high school participant stated that his parents were steering him to certain careers "because of their background and how they grew up. They grew up poor and they are looking for opportunities for their children to get into professions where they will succeed." Another youth shared the same opinion about her parents even though her father is a physician.

An Ivy League student, whose physician dad grew up less privileged, commented that her father was more forceful and stricter regarding academic and career achievement than her mom who grew up in a middle-class family in Nigeria. For many high-achieving second-generation Nigerian youth, such parental push towards certain careers complicated their decision to select a major in college. One youth noted that deciding on a college major was the hardest thing he had to do in his life, especially as he grew up believing he was going to be a doctor and had to face the pressure and disappointment of going home to face his parents when his educational plans changed. He admitted that it was painful for him to go home and inform his parents about his change of college major. He just was not interested in pre-med and had no passion for it. Meanwhile, he had already changed majors many times in the process of exploring and discovering what he really wanted to study.

The graduate student, who recently landed a job on Wall Street as an investment banker following an Ivy League graduate program, indicated that her parents were uneasy when she informed them that she was changing her major from pre-med to economics. She explained that her parents' uneasiness was due to the negative perception that Igbo people had about people in business because their scope of business was limited to import and export business. Some youth were determined to pursue their talents while keeping in mind the desire to satisfy their parents. One high schooler noted, "sometimes [parents] feel I should be going this way or that way, like in a certain profession—doctor, but I know my talents and what I want to do even though I might still get to the other things they want." He speculated that he might attend law school to satisfy his parents' desire for a trophy degree.

When asked to speculate on why Nigerians steered their children into certain professions such as medicine, law and engineering, the graduate school participant responded, "a part of the construct is being a professional and the ability to get a job in the United States and another is the status. The fact that many engineers in Nigeria prefix their names with engineer this or that, is a good example."

She further noted, "many Nigerian parents are fixated in careers such as medicine, law, and engineering and they get uneasy when their children do not go that route. I remember a Nigerian mother pleading with Nigerian parents to allow their children to study what they like and follow their interest." This participant was speaking from personal experience as she went through the switch from a pre-med program to economics. Her parents felt uneasy about her decision and she had to win them over.

According to one college participant, "It has been my experience as well as other second-generation Nigerian youth that Nigerian parents are demanding as far as what your goals should be and not allowing you to explore." In fact, this youth thought it might be interesting to explore the role of Nigerian parents in how second-generation Nigerian youth set their academic goals as a future study.

CHAPTER 5

Parental Factors

Parental Engagement

Research on the educational experiences of Black students often focuses on culture by examining parenting styles, language practices, parent-child interactions, and the value parents place on education and educational aspirations (O'Connor et al., 2007). However, the cultural lenses applied to these studies are from a white middle-class perspective, negating the variabilities in how different subgroups might opt to navigate the educational experiences of their children within their ethnic cultural milieu. For example, parental engagement to Nigerian parents may not look like the mainstream notion of parent engagement, as clear from this study.

Nigerian parents in the study were strategically engaged with the education of their children at home and at school. Their nature of engagement included traditional mainstream involvements in Parents-Teachers-Associations or the like and non-traditional (Nigerian-style engagements) methods. The level of direct school engagement varied according to parent's familiarity with the American educational system and cultural expectations with regards to the norms for parental engagement. Engagement also depended on the type of school the children attended and the personal motivation of the children.

Nigerian parents were engaged with the schools more frequently if the children attended a public school where it was easy to fall through the cracks or if the children were unmotivated. The nature of the parental involvement also ranged from direct homework and help with projects to just discussing schoolwork and the importance of education with their children.

Participants with younger siblings who were unmotivated and those whose siblings were in public schools observed that their parents were more actively involved and engaged with schools attended by their younger siblings. The oldest youth in the sample also reported that their parents were not actively engaged with their school when they were growing up but had witnessed an increase in the level of their parent's engagement with the education of their younger siblings. Participants attributed that to parental lack of understanding of the American educational system when they were growing up. The youth also reported that the nature and type of parental engagement decreased as they got older, gaining more maturity, and working in higher-level classes that required skills not readily available to parents. However, their parents still provided moral support and the motivation for the youth to thrive academically.

One high school participant who started out in an urban public school before moving to a suburban high school noted, "My mom was involved in PTA and was in contact with the teachers. Now [in his suburban high school], I think that I can take care of myself, but I tell them what is going on." During the interview with his mother, she confirmed his statements. She described her engagement with her children's education and school involvement as follows: "From kindergarten until my children finished primary school and going to high school, I was active in the PTA, and I was involved in activities in their school. I sneaked into their classrooms and checked with their teachers to make sure that they were doing what they were supposed to do. I also checked with the principals. I was reading to my children when they were young. They were able to read before they started Kindergarten. I still help them with the small knowledge I got. I still discuss their education with them."

This parent realized that she was unable to provide direct help with the assignments her children brought home in high school, so she supported her children in other ways. She indicated that when she discussed school with her children, she asked them about the type of homework they had and provided some input as needed. She believed that her active involvement and presence in her children's school helped her children to do well in school as she got to know the teachers, the principal, and other kids in her children's class. Her beliefs were shared by other Nigerian parents who suggested that their presence in the schools helped their children perform well in school. Nigerian parents believed that their presence in the schools made their children comfortable with their identity and they felt it was important for teachers to know that their children had supportive parents.

One mother who was engaged early in her children's school had this comment about her engagement and the value of her presence: "I visit their schools. From elementary school, Kindergarten to grade one, I took them to school. They need you with them. It builds their confidence to stay in school. I chaperoned school activities and did read-aloud for the elementary school ones. I attended most school activities though it is now tougher with my studies, I make sure that I do all I can do." This full-time mother and student went on to describe what she did to stay engaged with her children's education. "I supported them in their homework. At the beginning of each year,

I tried to know their teachers and relate with the teachers to let them know that I am one of the student's mothers. I get some of the syllabi and help my kids before they go back to school. I make my children understand the meaning of time management in life and to understand that one can never waste his time and to make effective use of time."

Another suburban high school youth, who also started in an urban public school, indicated that her dad was an active member of the Parent-Teacher-Association in her elementary school years, but her parents were not as involved in her high school years—although her mother was frequently in touch with the counselor so that they could talk about her child's education. Her school was a suburban one, but she also was attending a special inter-district science-and math-themed urban high school for a few selected students. She stated that her parents have left her to her "own devices" in high school. When her mother was interviewed, she pointed out that her daughter's high school did not encourage parental engagement and she would have liked to have been more involved.

During the mother's interview, she further elaborated that when her children were younger, both she and her husband were actively engaged with the education of their children. She noted, "With all of them, we made it a duty to be engaged. With the first and second ones, we lived in a city and we took the opportunity to go for their report card conferences—whether the kids were doing well or bad. We wanted to know their teachers and ask questions. Being that they were in football and the marching band in high school, I was involved in the band parents selling things at the concession stand at band events, did bake sales, and traveled with the group to competitions. With the third child, we moved to this suburb. We always struggled with the fact that they did not have conferences during report card season in this school district. You went at the beginning of the school year as a group for the open house, not a one-on-one basis and that was it. You are allowed a parent conference if your child is not doing well. That did not sit well with us. For six years, I went in for a parent conference for her. I do not think it is correct. To me, it was not a good idea even though my kid was doing well. I would have preferred to know the teachers. I did not have any interaction with the school in the last two years of her high school other than going to the early open house. I did not enjoy that. In the first two years in high school, she was in marching band and I went to parents' meeting but stopped after two years."

An Ivy League college youth who attended a parochial high school with her siblings indicated that her parents were "not necessarily involved in school but it was assumed that I had to do well, or something was wrong." One of her older siblings corroborated the statement, saying, "My mom always wanted to get involved but couldn't because she had to work. And my dad had to work, especially in elementary school when we had the Parent-Teacher-Association meetings. My mom had the intentions, but life was hard. But when she did come, she made her face known and everybody recognized her and knew who we were because there are so many of us." The parents placed their trust in the Catholic school to do right by their children.

During the interview of their mother, she reiterated what her daughters said, but indicated that whenever the schools called upon her for anything, she tried to respond. She explained that she was completely involved when her children were young and when she was a student and did not have to work. She had gone to perform cultural activities for her children's school and made sure that she went in to meet the teachers. One of her children summed up her school engagement with the following: "Basically, I have a large family. In general, my parents were not available. For parent-teacher conferences, they made sure they were there to meet the teachers and to see what we were doing." Their mom was strategic in the way she engaged with school and having all the children in one school made her life a little easy as a working mother with many children. She also used her school engagement to bring multi-cultural diversity to the school by sharing her culture with the school which made her children noticed by the school. Other parents shared how they performed during multicultural events at their children's school.

Some parents were not as engaged with their children's schools for other reasons. One participant who was the oldest of four children, as well as the oldest in the sample, pointed out that her parents did not understand how the American educational system worked initially. Thus, her parents often relied on her to lead the way. She was the one who researched better schools around her community and convinced her parents to send her to a top private Catholic school. As a result of her self-determination and self-motivation, her parents did not have to engage with her school directly. At a young age, her mother taught her self-reliance by asking her to use the dictionary whenever she asked her for the meaning of a word she read. This youth also pushed her parents to enroll her in a community college while she was in high school to challenge herself and maintain her class rank. She believed that because of her innate personality and drive to succeed, as well as the type of school she attended, her parents did not need to directly engage with her school. It was different for her younger siblings, who were attending a public school and were not as motivated; there, her parents were actively engaged to make sure her siblings were taking the required courses and being challenged in preparation for college.

This youth's experience parallels the experience of another participant who was also the oldest of four children. This youth stated that as the oldest child, she was a guinea pig for her parents. Her parents did not actively engage with her school in her younger years, but she has noticed a tremendous difference between her mother's engagement with the school during her tenure and that of her siblings. She attributed the increased parental engagement of her parents to the fact that her mom knows more about how the school system works from the experience of raising her. In addition, her siblings, who attended public school, were not as motivated as she was. She believed that the level of motivation of the child and the type of school the child attended mitigated the level of parent-school engagement of Nigerian parents. As she observed, "Public schools are bigger and it is easier to fall through the cracks, like taking regular courses rather than taking higher-level courses." So, her mother became more actively involved to make sure that the counselors did their job with regards to course selections and placement in college-prep classes.

This youth, who attributed her parent's lack of engagement to their being immigrants without a strong awareness of how the American educational system worked, explained how her mother has taken her experiences and parlayed them for the benefit of the Nigerian community around them. Her mother had not only become more engaged with the schools her younger siblings attended but instrumental in rallying other Nigerian parents in their school district to form a Nigerian parent's association to promote the interests of their children. This speaks to the power of knowledge and the ability of Nigerian parents to build social capital within their communities.

Non-school Parental Engagement

There were various ways that Nigerian parents engaged their children academically both at home and outside the home that were not visible or known to the schools. The non-school engagement was defined here as the ways that Nigerian parents engaged their children academically without the involvement of the schools. This can also be defined as the non-traditional parental engagement in the education of their children outside the realms of mainstream America. In addition to the expectation to do well in school, Nigerian parents supported their children to do well in school morally and financially; through home structure and routine; by providing enrichment education; and by being role models to their children. Having both parents at home was also a bonus, though the focus-group told me that "with Nigerians, one parent can do the trick." This response came up during the focus-group's discussion of single- parent and two-parent homes.

High-achieving second-generation youth talked about the importance of having routines and structure early in their lives. They also valued knowing that their parents were there to help them with their homework when needed. For example, one high school participant stated, "the routines I had, especially in elementary and middle school, helped. My dad always helped me with math and my mom always helped me with the science projects. They both used their strengths to build my character and work ethic, which taught me to work hard."

Some youth indicated that they did not need their parent's help with homework in high school, but their parents pushed them to do their best and taught them time management. For example, one youth indicated that she did not often need homework help from her parents but when she asked for help, her dad explained more than she ever needed. Another stated that other people who played a role in her academic success were her parents, by teaching her to manage her time. Her parents also taught her how to stay focused and determined and to always think of the future. Her younger brother explained that their father, a professor, always helped with math homework.

Home Structure and Routines

The youth had daily scheduled activities, and homework was built into their daily routine, along with house chores and extra-curricular activities. For example, two participants reported that their regular house chores made them more responsible than their peers. Their parents did not need to be home for homework to be done, as that was understood by all the youth. Clearly, Nigerian parents established routines and structure for their children. One parent noted, "I had some rules when they were younger. Before 8:00 pm, homework was done, and they had to go to bed early and get up early, especially when I was in school. That helped me to study when they were younger." She also indicated that in grades K-8, her children could not watch TV during the weekdays. Such rules became relaxed as the children got older. This mother admitted that her children were later able to stay up till 12:00 midnight. Her son mentioned during his interview that he stayed up till midnight or until his homework was completed.

One parent noted, "We did set the rule that after school was snack, nap (if needed) and homework, but you can't do homework past 9:00 pm except for if you had band practice or game. There was a rule that 9:00 pm was bedtime unless you had a game. By the time we were ready for dinner, homework was done, and we can check it and they could read for another half hour before going to bed."

Another parent explained her rationale for TV rules. "We looked at the hours that American kids watch TV, and it depends on how you were raised. You did not spend that much time on TV. From others, we knew, and we saw how many hours they spent on TV and felt it was not what we wanted our kids to do. We wanted to interact more with them rather than them sitting in front of the TV."

One Ivy League participant described the TV rules in her house this way, "In elementary school and middle school, dad had no TV days. Three of the five-week days, you picked maybe two programs you wanted to watch during the week. Dad did not like the values or rather, the lack of values portrayed on American television." Other youth shared similar TV rules growing up but added that even when they could watch TV, they did not have the time for TV, as they were often busy with other activities.

Another Ivy League student described the TV rules at his home as follows: "Basically, no TV was allowed when we were growing up but as I got closer to college-age, my parents became more relaxed with TV. It was obvious that at this point we knew how to handle ourselves and the TV will not interfere. We never really had a need for TV because we were always doing something. I was at basketball games or playing my game upstairs, especially during primetime shows. I was tired when I got home anyway unless it was the weekend." His mother validated his statement regarding the TV rule. She stated, "They just have to do all the homework above and beyond. When they were growing up, they were only allowed to watch TV on the weekends. During the week, when they finished their homework, they read. They could not isolate or lock themselves up to watch TV."

Another parent noted, "When they were young, I remember we had a rule on no TV during the week from Sunday to Thursday night because they need to focus on their study, homework, sports activities, and extra-curricular events at the school. During the weekends were not a problem and they could stay up to watch TV as long as you get up in the morning to do your chores." Her daughter who graduated high school as the valedictorian of her class in a suburban high school admitted during her interview that in high school, she spent a lot of time watching TV and had to get her homework done in school before she got home so she could watch TV. However, she admitted that high school was not challenging for her.

Financially, the youth acknowledged the support they received from their parents, which allowed them to excel in school. The oldest participant in the study acknowledged that even though she was self-motivated, her parents were incredibly supportive financially, as they had to get second jobs to pay for her private high school education. She stated, "my parents sacrificed a lot to put my siblings and me in private school. It was not easy for them being lower-middle-class background then. It was hard to pay for the education for my siblings and me and so my parents took extra jobs and sacrificed." Her parents also paid for her to take courses at the community college while she was in high school.

Another participant, who attended a suburban public K-12 school, acknowledged that her parents were supportive in paying for an Ivy education in addition to the types of support they gave her prior to college. For example, she indicated that her parents made sure that her homework and projects were done and took them to the library when needed. Even when her parents could not give direct help, like when she took calculus, they helped her indirectly with moral support and encouragement.

Some parents supplemented school assignments with parental assignments. For example, one participant remembered that when she was in the second grade, her mother passed along a science project from her high school teaching job. Her dad took her to the science and math institute, and to summer and Saturday enrichment programs in the sixth and seventh grades. As a result, she was always ahead of her classmates in middle school. For the youth that needed extra challenges, parents paid for college courses while the youth were in high school like the parents who paid for community college courses while their daughter was still in private high school, which they also paid for.

One participant recalled that her dad created writing assignments out of her summer activities. For example, she explained that if she was taking a swimming lesson in the summer, she had to research how to build and maintain a swimming pool. Some of the parents interviewed also indicated that they created "mom's assignments" to supplement the school's curriculum and to challenge their children. Another parent shared how she made school assignments more rigorous than the school expected and convinced her child's teacher to back her up as an ally. Nigerian parents were resourceful and creative when resources were scarce. One focus-group participant remembered one summer she and her siblings did not have anything to do because all the summer programs were too exorbitant for the family. Her parents hired her to teach her siblings. She designed a curriculum used to teach her siblings and received pay from her parents. She believed she learned responsibility from that experience.

Some youth sought out their personal enrichment programs when their parents were not knowledgeable. One high school student, the youngest in the sample, who recently moved to his current state of residence with his family, took on the lead to transfer to a health-themed magnet high school of their public school system and also found a Saturday enrichment program for college-bound youth in the city. He was able to visit many Historically Black Colleges and Universities (HBCU) through this Saturday enrichment program and credited this program as part of his motivation to achieve and ultimately chose to attend an HBCU for college.

Finally, high-achieving second-generation Nigerian youth indicated that their parents were their role models and that they emulated the work ethic of their parents. The oldest participant summed up what she learned from her mother with this statement: "My mom, she was going to college and working. When I was young, any time I asked her a question she told me to go and do it myself. 'Figure it out, look it up in the dictionary'." She indicated that such responses helped her to be independent and self-reliant. This experience was not unique, as all the mothers interviewed for this study attended college while they had young children, and some worked outside the home in addition to raising children and working toward a degree.

Parental engagement through motivation

Although Nigerian parents interviewed for this study held high academic expectations for their children, they utilized various approaches to motivate and support their children beyond routines and structures. They motivated their children to achieve by rewarding good grades and told them folk stories of success as passed on from their parents. They used folk stories about growing up in Nigeria to provide an alternate frame of reference for their children and to remind their children that life could be worse. When parents were asked how they motivated their children to do well in school, one mother, responded, "We usually give them money, financial rewards or take them to dinner or shopping. Let us say they wanted a game like Nintendo, we would say okay you did well in school so let us go and get the game you wanted. Most of the time, it was a financial reward and of course a big hug."

Upon further inquiries on the use of folk stories of growing up in Nigeria, this mother continued: "We tell them the entire story all the time. We tell them about what they have that we did not have, especially their dad. It has become a family joke. When they ask for something and I would say 'go to Dad,' my youngest would say 'either give to me or forget it because if I go to Dad, he will tell me about not having sneakers when he was growing up.'"

Another mother indicated that she used herself and her family as a model of success and was clear about her expectations. She stated, "Sometimes I would point out that certain jobs and positions would get you far. I told them about the value and the ability to make decisions and not be subjected to others pushing you around. Because they are girls, it was important to me that they don't depend on a husband."

One mother described her motivation strategy as follows: "We take them out for lunch, to the movies, give them money, and buy things they need when they do well in school. I talk to them and tell them that life was not easy for us growing up in Nigeria. I tell them that most of us that made it to the United States came from poor families and that we struggle to make it and do better than our parents. It is not that our parents were not talented enough, but they lacked the opportunity, and it is now their time to do it and take advantage of the opportunity they have. Like my mom, she is very smart but being a woman, her parents could not afford to educate her, and she always told me to do better. The children are supposed to do better than their parents and my children have the opportunity. I always tell my children what I learned from my parents and grandparents and that they have to focus on their education and not waste their time."

Another mother with two children in the study narrated the actions her mother took to keep her motivated as a young girl, which she narrated to her children. She described her mother's actions as follows: "When I was growing up at home [Nigeria], my mother used to take me to her workplace and show me the director and the top people and would tell me that they got there because of their education. She would also take me to the market and show me the people under the sun and she would say that they got there due to a lack of education and would tell me that it was my choice as to which one I would prefer in life. I use all these examples for my children. I also encourage them by giving them what they want. I do not want to say, "bribe them.""

The mother of three participants used a variety of motivation methods, including some of what the previous parents described. Her motivation strategies depended on the child's level of self-motivation. She noted, "some motivations we used included money or Broadway shows, but I set the expectations so high that there were few Broadway trips. They looked forward to our three-day weekend trips in our timeshare. It was not part of the reward, but I could say to them that we would cancel the vacation to get them working hard. The trip was something we know we had to do to get out of the city and relax. I used to give money to them if they get [a grade of 95% average or above in their classes] but as time went by, the kids became self-motivated, especially the older ones. For the younger ones at home, doing consistently well would make me do something like pay a bill for them."

The same parent indicated that as an educator, she learned from her colleagues that high schools were ranked for college admission purposes. As a result, she and her husband planned early on that their children would attend either the special public high schools (for example, the Math-and-Science-theme school) or Catholic schools as a preparation for a competitive college. She also stated that she advised her children to pursue careers in the sciences where minorities were underrepresented. She sought out enrichment programs for her children to participate in to give them a competitive edge.

Cultural Socialization

Cultural socialization refers to the process and the various ways through which these high-achieving second-generation Nigerian youth were introduced to Nigerian values and culture. Nigerian immigrants generally belonged to cultural associations and they brought their children to the cultural celebrations. Some parents took the culture to the schools their children attended as a means of getting their children to embrace their unique cultural heritage. One youth indicated that her desire to give back to the Nigerian community was inspired by attendance at Nigerian cultural events with her parents. These social events typically engaged in fundraising activities to help groups in Nigeria.

Some of the youth spoke of how they lived and embraced Nigerian culture without knowing it. They participated in various Nigerian activities and gatherings, including religious activities in the Nigerian Catholic community. Three of the youth were actively engaged in their mother's Igbo language and cultural program as counselors and dancers, and their circle of friends in their early years came from that group. This helped to close the gap of not having friends from school. They also attributed the Nigerian cultural socialization as being a critical factor in their approach and outlook to life and their drive to succeed. One of them stated, "there is a certain approach to education that is taught to the children regardless of the household they grew up in. They are taught that education is first. Everyone is going to be a doctor, engineer, or lawyer because they are the professions that are worth more and you are always going to have a job." The oldest participant in the study concurred with the following: "The Nigerian community focuses on doing well and distinguishing itself. They refer to what their children are doing because Nigerians are competitive. Every Nigerian parent wants to say they have a daughter or son who went to such and such a school."

One youth commented that second-generation Nigerian youth were socialized to achieve. She said, "I feel that because of our upbringing, education is so integral to an Igbo child's upbringing. We are predisposed to achieve because it is encouraged. I don't think it is a one size fits all as circumstances are different, but because of our upbringing, we tend to want to do well in school." She attributed the 'tendency' to do well among second-generation Nigerians to their upbringing and speculated that there was a correlation between the upbringing and outlook in life and academic pursuit among second-generation Nigerians. She further noted that "being Nigerian gave me a culture from which to jump off from. I was taught values and to value education. I learned to adjust. When I realized that I was ill-prepared for college in high school I did not jump. Rather I had to work harder." Such attitudes helped the youth persevere when faced with academic challenges.

Some youth discussed how exposure to Nigerian culture, which valued education, provided them with a foundation in life. One participant noted that Nigerian culture influenced her perspectives in life. She stated: "My culture had strengthened me. Igbo culture is strong. It has a lot of values. It has made me strong and has built my character to be tough and to be able to take the punches. I have learned not to cry over spilled milk. I have matured a lot in comparison to my friends." She also felt that exposure to older Nigerians helped her to mature as they used proverbs to teach her about real life. Another youth also extolled the value of Nigerian community and believed that the extended family found in those communities taught the children to work together and be proud of who they are.

One participant was a part of his mother's language and cultural programs and attributed his success in life to these Nigerian cultural activities. He spoke highly of the importance of exposing second-generation Nigerians to Nigerian culture, as it was a key component to his adjustment and success. He stated, "I encourage Nigerian parents to expose their kids to it [Nigerian cultural activities]. I see a few kids on campus that were not exposed to it and they look awkward around those exposed to the culture. When you are growing, at a certain age you realize that you are different from other Blacks because of your culture and your name and you accept it or reject it. Diversity is now celebrated, and professors ask you about your experiences and they love it. The [second-generation Nigerians] who weren't exposed want to learn it and they can't because it should have started early." He also commented that second-generation Nigerians need peers with a similar background in this "crazy world we live in." "Crazy world" here referred to a country often plagued by racism and anti-immigrant sentiments.

Another participant reaffirmed the need to teach second-generation Nigerian youth their culture and to involve the youth in Nigerian gatherings. She indicated that youth often felt left out in Nigerian events and she believed that the youth should be included and should be prepared to take ownership of Nigerian culture for the next generation. She emphasized the need to transmit the "mindset" that youth could achieve to second-generation Nigerian youth. She noted, "Nigerians in Nigeria don't feel inhibited. Even for Nigerians living in the United States, that mindset is transmitted, but it goes back to Nigeria where growing up in the majority is different from being in the minority." This youth felt that Nigerians do not allow anything or anybody to get in the way of their future. From the responses I received, it was evident that Nigerian culture was salient and part of their perception of academic experiences and self-image as students. They learned from their families and the Nigerian community that Nigerians excel academically, and they run with the belief and the high expectations for academic achievement.

CHAPTER 6

Nigerian Factors

Nigerian Identity

Researchers have demonstrated that ethnic communities and organizations play a vital role in helping second-generation youth develop ethnic pride and identity (Smith, 2008; Foley & Hoge, 2007; Sears et al., 2003; Kibria, 2002; Ethier & Kay, 1994). Nigerian identity development for the study participants was multidimensional and critical to their success.

Survey data for my study showed that most of the participants claimed a Nigerian affiliated identity, although many of them recognized the situational and contextualized nature of their identity during the interview. Twelve youth from the in-depth interview identified themselves as Nigerian-Americans, two as Igbo-Americans, and two identified themselves as Nigerians of Yoruba origin. However, participants used various identities to describe themselves during interviews. The focus-group used the following identities when discussing how they negotiated their identity: American, hyphenated (Nigerian-American), national origin (Nigerian), pan-ethnic minority (Black), ethnic Nigerian (Igbo or Igbo-American), and pan-continental (African). They negotiated identity through various contexts. These youth not only provided the multicontexts under which identity negotiations could vary but also provided rationales for their identity variabilities. Participants' identities developed because of their interactions with different contexts and with different people. For example, a high school participant who lived in a large urban city and attended public school there until he moved to a suburban school had experienced bullying at the hands of his peers who were African-Americans and he shared how his identification has evolved. "I see myself as a Nigerian. Through the years, things have developed in me, I feel I should be taking pride in where my parents came from. When I was younger, I saw myself as American, later as African-American (Black), and now as Nigerian. There are three or four Nigerians at my school, but I am the only Igbo."

Another participant, an Ivy League student, articulated her identity negotiations thus: "Ethnically, I identify myself as Nigerian-American. However, this answer depends on the social context in which I am asked the question. Racially, I identify as Black, which I never really have to assert or verify in conversation, since this is readily visible. However, when the question of ethnicity (which to me means culture and heritage) comes into question among Americans (regardless of their race or descent), I always make it clear that while I was born and raised here, my parents are from Nigeria and that that culture is where I draw upon my core values and principles. Usually, when talking to Blacks (at Ivy, anyway), I just say Nigerian because they understand that I am second-generation. I usually do not have to identify with a specific tribe when asked about ethnicity; unless the other person is Nigerian, and they ask because they cannot place my name. I find that people who are second-generation usually can only place names that are blatantly Igbo or Yoruba. Then I say that my dad is …, which is where my name comes from; but that my mom is Yoruba – and then I usually give them my Yoruba name as kind of verification of my being Yoruba. While I identify with being Yoruba more than being from [father's ethnicity] although in Nigeria, technically you would claim your father's side, that is just because there are more Yoruba people around to identify with. I don't really feel a strong loyalty to tribal identity; it's just more like a detail when people are curious."

For one participant in graduate school, contact with other young Nigerian-born youth opened her eyes to not only a new experience but an opportunity to embrace who she was in terms of her identity. Here is what she said: "In college, for the first time, I met other Nigerian youth my age that I did not have the opportunity to meet where I lived. I also met a diverse group of Nigerian youth, those who grew up in Africa [Nigeria] as well as those who grew up in the U.S. like me. It was interesting to see the perspective of those who grew up in Nigeria and to see that those students were normal and confident. I became more involved with African organizations and less with the mainstream. We did things centered on Africa. My sophomore year was a turning point for me, especially meeting Africans from Africa. Prior to that, it was just my family friends, but the children were not my age. There were maybe four Nigerian families similar in life stage as my family in terms of the ages of the children. We didn't live in the same area or neighborhood as Nigerians lack ethnic communities, but we usually saw each other about once a month at functions." For this youth, interacting with peers who grew up in Nigeria is a validation that Nigerians are not only smart, but are proud of their heritage, and unapologetic about their culture. This experience helped shape how this youth chose to identify herself. She was one of the two participants who identified as Igbo-American.

With regards to ethnic identity, here is what one participant whose mother ran an Igbo cultural school said: "I would say that I am Igbo-Nigerian. There has always been the issue of who do you identify with. My parents have raised me to recognize who I am. This is part of me that is important (i.e., Igbo-Nigerian identity). I identify as Igbo-Nigerian, especially as Igbo because our culture is distinct and unique." On the issue of American or African-African or Black, here is how one participant explained her choice. "Nigerian-American; to say Black wouldn't encompass what I am. Also, African-American is too broad, I do not feel like I am American and if I said American anyway, people would ask me oh, where did your name come from?"

This Ivy League college participant said this about his identity navigation: "Basically, my general conclusion is that I am Nigerian-American. It is great. My generation has gotten into that (i.e., accepted the Nigerian-American identity). There is a difference when we go to Nigeria and they try to relate to us, and our cousins call us Americans, and over here we are Nigerians. I am Igbo, but I say that I am Nigerian, especially at school we flow well [referring to the camaraderie of second-generation Nigerians of different ethnic backgrounds]. If we are fighting ourselves, how does it look to others? We want people to look at us and fear us [referring to the power in number]. Most of [my friends] were born here. You are born in this crazy country and you need people with your experiences. Out of the core of us 9, 4, or 5 are second-generation Nigerians. The guys gravitate towards each other and the others are surprised when we laugh about our common experiences. We share jokes about how we grew up. When talking amongst ourselves, the accent comes out more. Certain jokes and references require the accent. We will live off- campus next year (some second-generation Nigerians) and it is great, especially as it is getting down to the end and we have the same goals to graduate."

Although high-achieving second-generation youth in the study indicated that they were friends with African-Americans when possible, they primarily identified with Nigeria. They had met successful Nigerians through their parents and at school and they identified with Nigerians. One youth indicated that she drew her core values from her Nigerian identity, but that there are circumstances when she identified herself as Black or African-American. Some youth also believed that Nigerian identity was contextualized. For example, if they were among other Nigerians, they identified with their ethnic Nigerian identity (Igbo or Yoruba), but in the presence of other Blacks (including African-Americans and other second-generation youth from Africa and the Caribbean), they claimed Nigerian identity. To add to their contextualized identity, another youth observed that when second-generation Nigerian youth visit Nigeria, their cousins and other relatives refer to them as Americans but in America, they are Nigerians.

The focus-group participants at an Ivy League college supported what the other participants said about their identity negotiations as second-generation Nigerians and shed more light on how they negotiate their identities in various contexts as follows:

"It depends, if I am talking to other Africans, I say I am Nigerian but to the general public, I say I am Nigerian-American."

"I never use Nigerian-American, I assume which State I came from when people ask me. "I say I am from North Carolina, but my parents were born in Nigeria."

"For a survey, I say Nigerian, if identity is stated [required]. If they want to know my ethnicity or nationality, I will say Nigerian-American. If they want to know which state, I come from I say,

CA. Where are you from can mean two things. What state you live in or your cultural identity."

"I will say I am from upstate New York, but my parents are from Nigeria."

"I identified with what I did rather than who I was through building relationships with my teammates in sports. So, I identified outside of race and culture (racelessness)." This participant is biracial with one white parent and I wondered if that could have impacted this response. The same participant shared that he often relied on memories from Nigeria as he navigated his identity when he was growing up. One youth had explained that her identity affiliations varied according to the contexts and identified herself in various ways between her survey, in-depth interview, and during the focus-group interview with Nigerian-American being her preference. Moreover, she expressed frustration about those Nigerians who "reject or deny being Nigerian or deny Nigerian identity." This demonstrates that the ethnic identity development and the process is not static but rather multidimensional and shifts with time and context (Phinney, 1990; Waters, 1990). Habecker (2017) found that immigrant African youth in her study navigate multiple identities that are also contextual, as many of the youth in my study.

Nigerian Identity as social capital

Nigerians have a history of actively seeking higher education because of the perceived prestige and economic benefits that accrue from it (Ojiaku & Ulansky, 1972). Nigerian immigrants must have passed on the value of higher education to their children. High-achieving second-generation Nigerian youth in the study attributed their academic success to a Nigerian identity; this was evident in their identity preferences and how they perceived their Nigerian identity as an asset. Youth stated that Nigerian identity was critical to who they were and to their academic success. Although they acknowledged the contextualized nature of their identity, they attributed many positive qualities to Nigerian identity and credited their parents and the Nigerian community for their development of that identity. This is contrary to the negative image of Africa and Nigeria as often portrayed in the media. Although Kelly and Schauffler (1996) found that immigrant groups use shifting identities as a defense mechanism from stigma, that did not appear to be the case with second-generation Nigerian youth in my study. These young people understood the importance of identity and how it influenced one's views of life. They were keenly aware of the role of perceptions and the negative perceptions of African-Americans in the United States. One participant made the following comment regarding identity:

"I think identity has an impact on self-perception. Perception is important, and I think that is what holds African-Americans back. If you start thinking or become absorbed in the mentality that the whole system is against us, then you cannot succeed. If you have an identity aligned with the Nigerian mindset to succeed, you will. That is not found in African-Americans [stereotype]. You need a mindset that is focused on achievement. The mindset that the white people are against us, Nigerians do not have this. I feel that Nigerians coming from Nigeria feel they are capable of anything. They may not necessarily feel inferior though their behavior may say that; they don't feel they can't do chemistry or engineering or anything because they are Black." This view counteracts the centuries-old historical oppression of African-Americans and the accompanying media barrage of negative African-American portrayals that affect other groups. It also impacts how some second-generation Nigerians interact with and view African-Americans.

The oldest participant in the study shared her experiences regarding her Nigerian identity. She identified as Igbo-American on the survey and during the interview. When asked whether being Black or Nigerian was ever a problem for her in school, she responded, "I think being Nigerian has been an advantage, especially today. A lot of the job opportunities I have had are because I am Nigerian. I think there is discrimination against African-Americans in hiring, especially in investment banking, and Nigerians dominate that field (in comparison to African-Americans). For me starting in college, it was always an advantage to say I am Nigerian. People in America have an obvious bias against African-Americans. I feel that I get a positive response when I say that I am a Nigerian. I definitely feel that identifying as a Nigerian has been a professional advantage. I went for an interview with a Japanese bank and once they found out that I was Nigerian, one of the interviewers told me about a Nigerian he went to school with and how smart and intelligent the Nigerian schoolmate was. It is an image problem. Whites and Asians see Africans as being different from African-Americans. It is a problem of institutional bias in hiring."

She also noted that from personal experience, Nigerian immigrants live in either white America or black America unless parents sheltered the children, and that influences the academic achievement of second-generation Nigerian youth. She speculated that the low performing and "badly behaved" second-generation Nigerian youth tended to live in predominantly inner-city neighborhoods where they were exposed to poor African-Americans. She believed that the exposure of these second-generation Nigerian youth to non-Nigerian identity contributed to the poor academic performances of the youth. This youth's personal observation requires further exploration.

Perceptions of Nigerians as Academic Achievers

Some youth stated that being around Nigerians elevates expectations about their behavior. They have observed their parents, relatives, and family friends who did well and had internalized that being a Nigerian meant doing well in school. As one of the participants stated, "I am used to being around Nigerians and you are expected to do well."

Being around Nigerians meant exposure to progressive young and adult Nigerian role models, including the larger Nigerian community. One high school participant who recently moved from an urban public school to a suburban high school was visibly excited when asked if he considered Nigerians successful. He responded with a resounding "yes" and further elaborated, "Even at my school, there are four Nigerian kids, and they are doing well. One of them has been on the honor roll for four years and heads three clubs as the president. Another one is so smart and popular that everyone knows her by name. It is common with Nigerians. I see [successful Nigerians] at school, church, and the [Nigerian cultural conventions]."

High-achieving second-generation Nigerians consider other second-generation Nigerians successful in academics. All youth participants indicated that they knew some successful Nigerians through their parents. Five college youth indicated that in college, their knowledge base regarding Nigerians increased through contact with their second-generation Nigerian peers. The youths' perception of Nigerians and their academic prowess also changed because of the college experience. Contrary to the college-age youth in the in-depth interview who primarily attended Ivy League colleges, the focus-group who also attended a single Ivy League college believed that Nigerian youth were not particularly academically talented, as they did not stand out for academic performance on campus. However, they perceived Nigerians as academic achievers in terms of their numbers in the Ivy League colleges. The focus-group participants admitted that they were humbled by attendance to a top Ivy League college where all students come from the tops of their high schools, often with better preparation. They redefined their definition of academic performance in terms of enrollment at an Ivy League college, not grade attained. They were "A" students in high school but now the context matters when discussing academic performance and achievement.

When asked the question "Do you know any successful Nigerians and how did you meet them?" one youth responded, "I know successful Nigerians mostly through my parents. When I came here (Ivy college), I met even more, and I learned about what their parents do and how they are successful. Most of the other Nigerian kids that I talk to have similar experiences and conclusions as me, which is they know many professional and successful Nigerians no matter the part of the country they are from. So, I have just come to assume that perhaps many Nigerians all over the United States are generally well off and doing well. But I know of people, mainly second-generation Nigerians who have ended up in jail, or getting sent to military school or something similar; however, they usually seem to be the black sheep of the family and the rest of the family is doing okay. In most of the cases, the Nigerians are lower-middle-class, instead of the upper-middle-class that I consider myself to be a part of. However, they are still making a living and I would not consider them lower class, like living in section 8 [government subsidized housing] or something." This speaks to the issue that some second-generation Nigerian youth do not adjust well in America and do not perform well academically. This participant attributes these problems to the class differences and the socio-economic status of the parents.

In response to the same question, one participant attending an Ivy League college commented that he has observed a high proportion of second-generation Nigerians in elite colleges. When asked whether he considered Nigerians successful in academics, he chuckled and responded, "Most definitely! It is one of the biggest jokes and complaints at school. It has been said that when you walk into a room of eleven Black students on this campus, five or six are Nigerians, three are Afro-Caribbean, and the rest are [African-Americans]. It is a testament to our upbringing. It is not just at this Ivy League college but also in other colleges." It was evident from the responses to questions about the perception of Nigerians in academics that high-achieving second-generation Nigerian youth had positive associations with Nigerian identity. Such perceptions came from participants' exposure to Nigerians through their parents, extended family, family friends, meeting other second-generation Nigerian youth, and exposure to the Nigerian community.

Extended community influence on motivation: It takes a village

Child-rearing is an important and collective task in the traditional Nigerian society involving immediate, extended, and the entire community (Onwujuba & Marks, 2015). I have observed that since they lack ethnic neighborhoods in the diaspora, Nigerians abroad recreate such communities through their professional, gender, ethnic, national, and religious group associations. Second-generation youth cited the role of their parents, Nigerian culture and community, and other second-generation Nigerian peers as having influenced them in their high expectations and self-motivation to achieve in school. Many of the participants have older siblings who have done well academically, and they have college-educated parents that are mostly professionals. In addition, they have been exposed to Nigerians who are doing well academically in various Nigerian gatherings, school settings, and through their family connections. This communicates to the youth that they can accomplish because they have seen what is possible at a close range.

A participant had this to say: "You need people around you that support you. Honestly, I am not doing it alone. It is my community, family, brother, sister, Igbo and Nigerian Community." He continued: "It is a combination of my environment, my cousins, my extended cousins, and the Nigerian community. A lot of them are lawyers, doctors, married and successful. I do not want to compete or outshine them; I just want to be successful for me. My classmates also help me to do my best." He shared with exuberance and excitement the impact of seeing other second-generation Nigerians who are doing well in his school. He also shared his perception of the Nigerian community in America with this statement: "I like the Nigerian community and community groups. I may not see them all the time, but I see them as a community. Even though it is hard to cooperate sometimes, we dance, sing, pray together. It is the extended family that teaches the children to work together and to be proud of who you are."

Here is what this participant said about the influence of her family and community on her aspirations and goals.

"Growing up, there was a lot of focus on educational achievement—academic success. Both my parents have graduate degrees (postgraduate) and the emphasis was on academic achievement. It was ingrained in us; it was also due to intrinsic motivation. I am goal-oriented, ambitious and I have a personality growing up that was bound for success. Lastly, I have always been motivated by the idea of giving back to the community. I got that through our town conventions. I have a need to be successful to give back to Nigeria.

My parents are part of a family that stayed abroad. My dad is one of nine men educated abroad and the rest went home. The uncles and relatives always say to me, 'You will come home to teach.' This is part of what motivated me."

Many Nigerian parents are schooling, working, and parenting at the same time. As a result, they taught their children independence and self-reliance. One participant spoke about how she became self-driven and motivated.

"My mom, she was going to college and working. When I was young, anytime I asked her a question, she told me to go and do it myself, 'Figure it.' 'Look it up in the dictionary' because maybe she did not know the answer herself but that helped me to become more independent. I also helped at home more than other [non-Nigerians] kids. It helped with creating a strong work ethic. I developed independence early in age."

This participant who credited her parents and ethnicity for her motivation said this:

"My parents have always been supportive of me in school. It was part of my upbringing. Being Igbo-Nigerian, school was integral. They understood that education is the key to success in this country and they are 100% supportive..." "I feel that because of our upbringing and because education is so integral to an Igbo child's upbringing, we are predisposed to succeed because it is encouraged. I do not think that it is a one size fits all, as circumstances are different. But because of our upbringing, we tend to want to do well in school."

Sometimes, parents used older siblings to motivate the younger ones. For example, one participant noted, "My younger sister was considering taking Chinese, but my parents told her to take Spanish instead, after conferring with my brother and me. My parents sometimes use the older sibling to talk to the younger ones."

Here is what one parent said about her older children motivating the younger ones. Her older children attended parochial school, but the younger ones are attending a magnet school and she is relying on her older ones for support of the younger ones. She said, "The youngest one never went to a Catholic school, but the influence of the older ones rubs off on her. My oldest daughter has taken over and they all listen to her. She does not talk much, but she is like a god in her quiet ways. My youngest one looks up to the older ones and adores them. The influence that the older ones got from the Catholic school is showing in the younger ones."

One youth summed it up this way, "Overall, it is the family history. Education is the key here…, it is always about school. We are addicted to doing well." "The family history" referenced here is the larger Nigerian family. Everyone in the community contributes to the achievement orientation and parents raise their oldest children with the expectation that they too become role models for their younger siblings.

CHAPTER 7

School Contexts and Experiences of the Study Participants

Several factors play a role in how young people perform in school. School context is one such factor (Griffin & Alexander, 1978; Ianni, 1989; Raudenbush & Bryk, 1989). Schools also play an important role in shaping the academic self-efficacy of students since they spend a large part of their lives in school with teachers. A major goal of this study was to identify the influence of school factors on the academic outcomes of high-achieving second-generation Nigerian youth. Four school factors were identified: relationship with peers, relationship with African-American peers, relationship with teachers, and relationship with guidance counselors. I will describe how second-generation Nigerian youth navigated relationships with their peers in general and their relationship with African-American peers as their proximal host group in America. Some of the youth in the study had an antagonistic relationship with African-American youth.

Research suggests that proximity and interactions with proximal host groups can negatively impact the academic outcomes of second-generation immigrant youth (Fordham & Ogbu, 1986). As Blacks, African-Americans is the proximal group for Nigerian immigrants, based on how people are categorized in America (Mittelberg &

Waters, 1992). Second-generation youth experience upward or downward mobility depending on their proximal host groups (Portes & Rumbaut, 1990; Portes & Zhou, 1993). However, this is predicated on the assumption that immigrant minorities have a single pathway to assimilation to the dominant host country based on the experiences of the European immigrants in the past (Bourhis et al., 2010). For urban-dwelling second-generation Nigerian youth in the study, their parents were proactive and opted for parochial and magnet schools which reduced the exposure of their children to negative influences from proximal hosts. Most of the youth in the in-depth interview group resided in urban areas but attended parochial or magnet schools for self-selected high-achieving students. In addition to a chance to a decent education with an emphasis on good behavior, attendance to parochial schools also allowed second-generation Nigerian youth to tap into the school social capital available to church members with community ties to the church (Parcel et al., 2001). While enrollment in parochial and magnet school distanced high-achieving second-generation Nigerian youth from low achieving proximal hosts, it did not shield the youth from peer teasing. Nigerian parents in the study also restricted their children from making friends in the earlier grades to reduce exposure to negative peer influence on the youth.

Relationship with Peers

Bronfenbrenner and Morris (1998) postulate that in addition to psychological factors such as academic self-efficacy and intellectual self-control and family factors such as having an adult at home who is involved with the child's education, peer relationship is another vital factor that influences children's academic performance. Experiences with and proximity of peers of all races influenced how second-generation Nigerians navigated peer relationships and with whom they associated with, including motives for picking their friends. Students who exhibit academic achievement tend to have peers who also value academic success (Kindermann, 1993). The youth in the study realized the value of peer relationships even when they did not always get along with some of their peers. For example, one youth who was frequently teased in the elementary school in an urban primary school for being Black, tall, and smart stated, "Classmates will save you when it comes to projects, homework, and they can explain it to you. You need to make strong connections and bonds even though you are not on the same level as them, but you need to associate with them." He admittedly had friends from a diverse background (African-Americans, Asians, Whites, and Hispanics), but he also admitted that he did not trust anyone as a close friend because of the history of teasing he endured in his younger years.

The youth selected their friends predominantly from peers with similar backgrounds such as second-generation backgrounds and from within the same classes they were enrolled in. One youth who attended a parochial high school reported that "my school is very diverse, and my friends include four or five Nigerians, majority second-generation Nigerians, and some are African-Americans." But she also indicated that she did not make friends until she got to college. Prior to college, her friends were often in the same classes and were competing with her for grades. Her parents restricted her socialization with classmates, and she could not go over to their friend's house or for sleepover parties. She related that her siblings had the same experiences.

On the contrary, her brother described his experiences differently and was proactive to avoid being picked on by peers. He stated, "My primary group of friends were the honors group. I understood early while going to school in …, where kids were mean, that quiet ones got picked on all the time. When I saw new kids in school, I reached out to them and invited them to join a club; they would stop feeling lonely. I find it easy to make friends. As my friends would say, I find it easy to slip into people's lives. I feel like friends are vital in each stage of life and especially people sharing the same stage of life with you." Another youth stated that prior to meeting other second-generation Nigerian youth in college, she tended to associate with other second-generation youth from the Middle East, Asia, India, and Jewish peers.

The attraction for the circle of friendship for high-achieving second-generation Nigerian youth in the study was that their friends were often in the same classes, which were honors and AP classes. This mitigated their interaction with groups who would pick on them for being academic achievers. Their friends were also in the same sports and clubs and often from a minority group, although they indicated that they got along with everyone. As one youth stated, "I did have three friends. We were in all honors classes. I was friendly with everyone. It was a small school and I got along with everyone." Another stated, "my closest friends are from freshman year because we were in the same classes, but we are not in the same classes this year."

Others stated that their friends were Indians, Latinos, Whites, Blacks, and Asians, African-Americans, Jamaicans and Haitians (second-generation). They found ways to navigate their peer circles.

Relationship with African-American peers

Second-generation Nigerian youth in the study identified themselves primarily as Nigerian-Americans, Nigerians, or by their Nigerian ethnic origin while understanding the contextualized nature of identity. Clearly, they knew that they were racially Black and were aware of the negative perception of African-Americans in American media and society; and avoided behaviors that would portray them adversely. Three youth participated in the African-American Club where African clubs did not exist and were friends with African-American youth who shared similar academic aspirations.

One Ivy League youth, who counted some African-Americans as her friends in high school, while being teased by other African-American girls, described her high school interaction with African-American peers as follows: "My high school was two-thirds white, 30% Asians and very few Latinos. The first two years, it was 20% Black and then with neighborhood redistricting due to overpopulation at another local high school, it became 5% Black in a county that is a 25% Black population. The Blacks sat together in the cafeteria, dressed in baggy clothes, braids, nails with extensions, and [spoke] loud. Of course, this was not representative of every Black person at my school, but a few of them were. And of course, this behavior is very salient in a school of racial composition like we had. It is not that I was not proud to be Black, I was friends with them on an individual basis, but I just did not sit at the table with them in the cafeteria or wear the same things. I was on the executive board of the African-American Awareness Club as secretary and treasurer. I code-switched in speech patterns and dressing sometimes. I dress up more when I know I am going to something with a lot of Black people [African-Americans]. I won't dress up for … [African Students Club], but I will for a Black Students Union meeting [African and African-America group]."

Another youth, who attended an elite Catholic high school, described her relationship with African-American youth as follows: "With African-Americans, I did not grow up with them prior to college. I never felt like I could hang out with them, but now as I got older, I do, especially from a professional perspective for networking.

I did not like the Black Students Union. We shared a common area, the quad, and a common dining area, though I did not live in the [Black resident hall]. I could not relate to the African-American culture. I was struggling with where I fit in, with the Whites I spent 12 years of my life with, with the [newfound] African group with whom I shared heritage with, or with the African-Americans. I now had a choice and I gravitated toward African students. Also, as a group, Africans did not associate with African-Americans. There was tension between the African Students Union and the Black Students Union because the population of African students was growing and the African-Americans took notice. A lot of second-generation Igbo youth joined the Black Students Association because of the elitism of the African Students Association members and so [second-generation Igbo youth] joined the Black Students Association and could identify with African-Americans, especially if the Igbo youth attended an urban high school in the United States."

This is interesting in the sense that some high-achieving second-generation Nigerian youth who grew up in urban areas identified with African-Americans at this elite college on the West Coast because they perceived the African group—dominated by Nigerian-born ones to be elitist. The Nigerian-born students would have come from wealth as children of the elite class in Nigeria and grew up with housemaids and could not relate to the black experiences in the United States. Clearly, this was a class conflict between the groups based on their backgrounds.

Two high-achieving second-generation Nigerian youth negotiated their identity across multiple social terrains. One indicated that she knew that she was Black and could identify herself as African-American under certain circumstances. She developed a strategy to cope with her multiple identities by code-switching. In the presence of her African-American friends, she spoke Black English to gain in-group status with her African-American peers.

Another youth who attended a high school where she was the only Black in her class concurred that second-generation Nigerian youths' relationship with African-Americans was influenced by whether the youth grew up in an urban setting and hence were exposed to African-Americans or not. In her case, she had limited contacts with African-American youth during her high school career and chose her friends from teammates.

Relationship with Guidance Counselors

The relationship that high-achieving second-generation Nigerian youth in the study established with their guidance counselors varied. It was dependent on the type of help youth sought, as well as the type of school where they sought it. Some students pushed their guidance counselors to meet their needs in schools the counselors did not necessarily understand the process of applying to an elite private college due to the lack of applicants the school produced in the past. One youth was proactive in befriending her new guidance counselor ahead of senior year to gain future access. Regarding course selection and tracking, the youth reported that because they were on track for honors and Advanced Placement (AP) classes, their academic track was pre-programmed. As a result, the counselors did not have to do much to influence them. Two youth reported that they did not have the need to make use of their guidance counselors. For example, one indicated, "Teachers recommended us for what level of courses to take—AP, Honors, or regular. The guidance counselors usually follow the teacher's recommendation, but your parents can override the recommendation. It has never happened to me because I am always in AP and honors classes. In ninth grade, the English honors class was full, but my counselor put me in it anyway because I would be bored in a lower-level class."

When youth were asked if their guidance counselors helped them with course selection and college preparation, one youth stated, "I didn't really feel much need to use them. There were four counselors for 1526 students. I started talking to my counselor more when applying for college and scholarships. I do not know if the counselor treated me differently as a Black because I was doing well. Also, I don't know if they treated me differently from other students because I wasn't there when they interacted with those students." She also pointed out that as the most qualified Black student in her senior year, based on her Preliminary Scholastic Assessment (PSAT), Scholastic Assessment Test (SAT) and Grade Point Average (GPA), her counselor nominated her for several awards and scholarships, but she could only get those that were merit-based.

Another participant who attended an elite private high school with a favorable student-guidance counselor ratio reported a better guidance counselor relationship. She noted, "we had a school counselor assigned to us in the ninth grade and a career counselor in the sophomore and junior year. It shows how involved the school was and the attention it gives to the students. You had to apply and interview to be able to get into the school. There were plenty of resources available for a school population of 380-400 students."

Although the students reported that they were pre-tracked for honors and AP classes, whatever guidance counselor help they did need, however minimal, did not always come. Three of the students who attended urban magnet and urban parochial high schools reported that their counselors were not helpful. An urban magnet high school attendee, reported, "The counselor assigned to me was not helpful, but other counselors within my house were helpful. The combination of the three counselors within my house helped. The other counselors were always there when I needed them." Another youth, who attended the same high school, stated: "I don't really like my guidance counselor because the only time I have spoken to him is when I needed to change my class and I don't think he was helpful to me."

Two youth who reported favorable relationships with their counselors were proactive and prompted the counselors. Four youth who attended the same urban parochial high school reportedly had to push their counselors for what they needed. One of them stated, "in my school, which didn't have a lot of kids, the seniors typically went to local colleges, so going away to college wasn't the emphasis. I had to press the counselor for a lot of things. I had to seek her out and pull the information out. The counselor was not bad, just that it was not typical for kids at this high school to want to go out of state for college or to apply to an Ivy League college. The counselor was not progressive, but now it might have changed because I, my brother, and my sister have gone to an Ivy League college from the school. The counselor may see that she needs to be outgoing since we went to an Ivy League college from this high school."

Her younger sibling who attended the same high school had a different experience and noted, "[The counselor] went the extra mile with me. I remember the time I came in with an application that was due in three days and she had it ready the same afternoon. That is why I said it was unfair earlier [counselors helping high-achieving students more than low-achieving students]. Preference is not necessarily great because it was helpful to some but unfair to others. In talking to other students in high school, some of the students said that their counselors were not really pushing them. Even some of the students that I met in college have said that the only reason they made it to an Ivy League college was because of themselves. If they had not pushed themselves, they wouldn't have made it to the Ivy college."

His younger sibling who also attended the same school and reported a different experience stated, "We had two counselors, one for the freshmen and sophomores and one for the juniors and seniors. In my freshman year, I did not know the counselor assigned to me. I used to talk to the other counselor for juniors and seniors, but she left after my junior year. I was concerned that her replacement would not be able to know me to be able to write a good college recommendation, so I sought her out and befriended her. As a result, she came to recognize my face and know me and whenever new information about scholarships came in, she told me. She gave me great opportunities to get scholarships."

Another youth who attended the same parochial high school as the three siblings shared a different experience, which suggested that counselors have not changed as one of the graduates predicted. This shy participant who was equally motivated and was third in her graduating class reported, "We had two guidance counselors in high school, one for the freshmen and sophomores and one for the juniors and seniors. My counselor was not necessarily helpful. I kind of did everything for myself. She helped me to narrow my college choices and that was it. I remember when I told her that I wanted to go to this college. She said the only people that she had seen get into this college were the valedictorians and the salutatorians, but I was third in my graduating class." It appeared that the three siblings were more assertive in pursuing the guidance counselors to get what they wanted.

One youth summed up the relationship between guidance counselors and high-achieving second-generation Nigerian youth by explaining his relationship with his counselor: "She's helpful when I go to ask questions but would not put out stuff or helpful information on scholarships out for you. They are not proactive. You have to seek out information from them." That was precisely what many of the youth in the study had done. They sought out guidance counselors whether they were assigned to them or not. They were also proactive, creating their relationship with the counselors and making the counselors take notice of them. They challenged guidance counselors to see unlimited opportunities for their students and to see what is possible for Blacks and students from immigrant families. The youth refused to take no for an answer and refused to be discouraged from pursuing their dreams with or without the help of the school guidance counselor.

Relationship with Teachers

High-achieving second-generation Nigerian youth reported a favorable relationship with their teachers. They did not perceive teachers as being against them probably because they excelled in their schoolwork and they were raised to respect adults. This was a recurring theme from my interview with the parents; that they insisted that their children must be respectful of the teachers and other adults at school. Youth indicated teachers were supportive of their schooling, although two also reported having some unresponsive teachers. However, those youth did not perceive the unresponsive teachers as personally targeting them. Youth also realized that establishing a good relationship with teachers was important. For example, one youth who reported that most of his teachers had been supportive, stated, "Most of the teachers have been supportive but they pick favorites, and some are not actively involved with students, but overall, they have been supportive. I feel that having a good relationship with teachers and classmates is important. Teachers are grading you."

Some youth spoke of the special bonds they formed with their teachers in the parochial elementary school they attended. Such bonds left impressionable imprints on the minds of the youth. One of them ecstatically recalled her relationship with some of her teachers. She described her experiences as follows: "I had really great teachers. My first-grade teacher, she was great. I think I remember I was doing something bad, like talking in class and she gave me a mean look. It reminded me of my mom, and I stopped. My second-grade teacher, [Mr.], I keep in contact with him and I send him cards. All the teachers we had were instrumental to our success. We all went to the same school. Since we are a large family, teachers knew us, and we were good kids. My eighth-grade teacher was great." When asked to elaborate on what made her eighth-grade teacher great, she added, "She was instrumental in helping me adjust to my new school. She made history so interesting, relevant, and alive. She taught us poetry and I was not a fan of poetry and I never read poetry, but she made it fun and interesting. Since she taught us many subjects, I feel I learned a lot from her."

A high school senior in the study indicated that teachers and staff had been supportive from early on in her schooling career. She stated, "Since Pre-K to last year teachers have been supportive not only in the classroom but outside. I have cultivated a strong support group amongst the faculty, staff, principal, and counselors. I went to them at times of need." Her principal also nominated her to the state board of education where she represented the voice of youth in her state at her state Capitol.

Three youth indicated that given the type of school they attended and their drive to do well in school, teachers had no choice but to be supportive. One who attended a small elite Catholic school, explained, "I went to an exceptionally good high school, a private Catholic school for girls. The setup is one with a lot of individual attention to students. If I were struggling, though that was not the case, there was help, but in my case, their goal was to challenge me, and they did. The student-teacher ratio was favorable."

One youth who was the valedictorian of her senior class stated, "My teachers were incredibly supportive. If teachers have students who are motivated and thirsty for knowledge, teachers have no choice but to support them. I have had some teachers who were not interested or supportive, but it was not personal to me. Even now, I have some professors who have been supportive and helping me to see that education is important."

Her younger sibling related his experience with teachers: "I would say yes, for a lot of teachers, because some kids do not want to try, when teachers see kids trying, they grab them. It became a complaint in the junior year when everyone was trying to work on the college application. The top 10 students were getting a priority, but the others were forgotten or had something missing from their files after the due date. I appreciated it, but at the same time resented it because those kids were also trying to go to college. The English teacher was my favorite. She told me about the Ivy League schools. I remember her saying that the Ivy League was overrated in this country and around the world, but an Ivy education can allow you to get into places. That was the reason I chose to attend an Ivy League college. I could have gone to a state college on a free ride."

All youth reported that overall, they had good teacher relationships and most of their teachers were supportive. But they also recounted negative teacher experiences. For example, one youth who graduated from a suburban high school described her experience with teachers as follows: "Yes, for the most part [teachers] were supportive. A teacher recommended me to skip a grade in elementary school. In elementary and middle school years they were supportive, but in high school they were indifferent. Maybe because of the student's age, they relied on the student's motivation. In a few cases, the teacher thought I was a typical Black kid. For example, in my senior year in high school, I was taking five AP classes out of the possible seven and needed to drop one to do independent research. Before I dropped one, I had a difficulty in AP chemistry. We had to take this one quiz and keep taking it until you get 10 out of the 10 questions right. By the fifth time I got 9 out of 10 and was frustrated. The teacher said to me, 'you may not be able to handle everything we do in this class during the year.' Although he did not say it directly, I could tell he did not have a high expectation of me, probably because I was Black. Although other kids were still taking this quiz, I do not know if he told them that they could not handle it. When I told him that this was my fifth AP class because I knew that he was thinking that I was a low achiever, he then looked at me with a surprised look. He realized that it wasn't that I wasn't capable, but instead that I was doing too much."

In conclusion, high-achieving second-generation Nigerian youth had a positive relationship with their teachers in the lower grades. One youth indicated that they encountered low teacher expectation and apathy on the part of some teachers in the upper grades but that was not representative of the group. One notable observation was that youth who attended urban parochial schools felt supported by their teachers but in college, they also reported being underprepared for the rigors of Ivy League colleges even as they graduated at or near the top of their classes. A study of second-generation Nigerian youth in urban public schools would shed more light on what their experiences are in urban schools and would yield more accurate data on the school factors and experiences of second-generation Nigerian youth.

CHAPTER 8

Challenges of High-Achieving Second-Generation Nigerian Youth

Survey data revealed that high-achieving second-generation Nigerian youth had challenges primarily in the social and peer relationship domains. Five youth reported challenges in each of those areas, two reported academic challenges, with one participant reporting teacher or staff challenge. Those social problems were specifically related to peer teasing, under-preparation for college, the racialization of success, and parental pressure. One youth reported that she perceived low expectations from one of her teachers and mentioned a fear of her accomplishments being racialized or viewed only through the prism of her race rather than attributed to her efforts. Another youth in the focus-group also mentioned racialization of his success as an attempt to discredit his efforts.

Although two participants identified academic challenges as difficulties on the survey, six participants talked about these challenges in interviews. The academic difficulties they discussed were primarily addressed under-preparation for Ivy League colleges. Of the seven youth participants who resided in an urban setting and attended parochial schools, five of the youth talked about the challenges of dealing with the academic rigors of competitive colleges, despite their stellar academic records in the urban parochial schools they graduated from. When the issue of choosing a major in college came up during the focus-group interview, two participants indicated that they selected their majors after having trouble in the pre-med track. Despite their demonstrated academic achievements, urban parochial schools did not adequately prepare some of the youth for the rigors of Ivy League colleges. Yet they persevered. This was a significant issue since many of the youth aspired to careers in pre-med and other challenging fields.

Peer Teasing

Several participants reported that they were teased in school and the teasing came from Blacks as well as white students, regardless of the setting, whether public or private, urban, or suburban. The youth recognized that peers were instrumental to their success in school and they attempted to shield themselves from bruising conflicts. One participant was proactive and projected himself visibly as a leader to avoid peer teasing. He indicated that he would often approach new students and offered to help them out by introducing them to various school clubs. He also reported that he participated in several activities and hung out with smart and popular kids to shield himself from potential bullies. All the youth indicated that they limited their peer selection to students from their classes and activities, as well as those with similar immigrant backgrounds, to avoid peer teasing.

Youth were teased for various reasons. Three youth were teased for being too young, too tall, for "acting white", and for other reasons, depending on the environment they grew up in. One participant who grew up in a suburban upper-middle-class family stated that even though she got along with her peers in middle school, she was teased for many reasons. She reported: "I was teased by kids in my classes for being younger than other kids [after the fifth grade but not for academics since she was in a gifted class with other gifted students]. Other Black kids teased me for being too white [her accent and dressing]. It was a suburban school outside the District of Columbia, which has changed from a mostly white to a more diverse school district. However, the particular school was mostly white."

When asked to elaborate on being too white, she responded with the following, "I think it was my accent. Over the years I have learned to talk differently and have learned to switch back and forth depending on whom I am talking to. Also, my dress, I did not dress in the black fashion that [other Black students] wore when they teased me for being too white. They had braids and my hair was relaxed and straight. One of these three girls that particularly liked to tease me ended up getting expelled from our school. The main group of students I hung out with in middle school was mainly from the minority group—one Nigerian, one Haitian, one African-American, one Vietnamese, one Chilean, one Jewish, and two white students. Of the Blacks in my group, we were the higher-achieving Blacks. We were in the gifted and talented classes together and the other Black girls that teased me were in the regular classes." Another participant shared a similar experience when she described her experience as follows: "In high school, I didn't get a lot of comments from Whites but from African-Americans, because I was in Advanced Placement and Honors classes. They would comment that I was taking AP classes, talked differently, and had parents with accents. But here at [Ivy league college], I felt racism, but it may be due to economic differences between students here."

Another youth, who attended a public urban elementary school and urban magnet elementary and middle school before moving to a suburban high school, described some of the teasings that he endured as follows: "I was made fun of because I am Black and tall. People have stereotypes and call you names. People can be judgmental. When you say the wrong answer or make a mistake, they make fun of you. When you make friends with one group, the other group will make fun of you. But people are always going to make fun of you for one reason or the other. When I was young, I wanted to be cool and be looked up to. Now all I care about is getting my work done, doing what I have to do." The youth also acknowledged that his teasing was due to a combination of factors. He added, "It is the combination of being Black and tall. Some see me as fitting in with white people because I am smart. That should not get to me because there is always something people will not like about you. It could be anything. I don't let it get to me." This is a lot of wisdom from a young person. Another youth who was a high school senior in an urban school, described her experiences with being teased as a young person as follows: "When you are younger, you get teased because you're African, but the school was diverse and if you pick on people you get picked on too. In freshman year, you got picked on because you are African, but it wasn't a problem because I embraced my culture and people accepted."

Focus-group participants also experienced teasing in school. Four of them were teased for various reasons: "acting white," being in AP classes, African name, clothing style, being biracial, and being too young. One of them shared her experiences with peer teasing as follows: "I grew up in the Midwest. I lived near a university and some kids came to our school from … in junior high school. You know African-Americans had their way of talking and I had my way of talking which African-Americans considered to be white. So being Black and of Nigerian background and I was in higher-level classes, one African-American called me an Oreo and I was livid. I said to her that if anything, I was more Black than you." Another youth shared her experiences with both her African-American and white classmates. She stated, "I got Ebola [because it rhymed with her name] a lot and I didn't know what Ebola was until another kid told me. White kids called me medusa [referring to a monster from a Greek Mythology with snake hair because participant often wore her hair in braids, a style unfamiliar to the white classmates]. I had no other Blacks in my academic class, but I was in the band with other Blacks; the school was 92% white." The experiences of the youth were unique because they fell victim to both Black and white peers and their socio-economic status could not shield them from racism or bullies. Although the youth shared experiences of being victimized by peers, they did manage to persevere and thrive academically in the face of peer teasing and bullying.

High School Under-preparation for College

All youth in the study attended parochial or magnet schools in an urban area or suburban high schools. Although they were in honors and AP classes in all their academic courses, three out of the four college youth who attended the same urban parochial high reported that they were ill-prepared for the academic rigors of Ivy League colleges even though they graduated at or near the top of their class. Additionally, some youth reported that they did not really need to know how to study in high school, therefore they did not cultivate good study skills in high school. Yet they excelled anyway because they were able to "ace" the high school tests and quizzes without studying. One youth described the impact of his lack of good study skills on his first year in college succinctly: "In high school, you didn't need to study. It was just go to class, take a test, and ace it. I did not study. I just did the required assignments. Studying was foreign to me until I got to college. In high school, if anything, when we have a game or an activity with my classmates, we get on the bus and did homework.

In our class, my friends and I were in the top seven. If we studied, we could have done better. We could have been the valedictorian and the salutatorian. My two sisters understood that and studied, and both were the valedictorian. And we went to the same high school; until college, I realized what studying meant and that studying meant locking yourself up for three to four hours. It didn't happen in high school."

As a follow-up question, I asked the youth how he made up for his lack of study skills, to which he responded, "My first semester in college was my worst ever, academically, socially, and culturally. It was terrible. I did poorly because I did not understand what studying was. I could not do a shift suddenly to go from not knowing how to study to studying. The process takes a long time. I did so poorly my first semester I was on academic probation and I could not understand why. I did not know how to do it properly, how to get into the mood, and how to retain what I studied. So, I let my friends distract me and when they said let us hang out since they were done studying, they thought I was done. Because studying was driving me crazy, I would hang out with them. I was a party king and knew all the party information instead of studying. I had so much 'free time' due to not studying and I found ways to occupy myself. If anybody needed information about a party, they would call me."

Although the youth indicated that both his siblings, who were valedictorians of their senior class, understood what studying meant, both siblings also reported that they were under-prepared for college in their parochial urban high school. This raises the issue of the ability of the urban parochial school they attended to adequately prepare their students for the rigors of competitive college. One youth who graduated from the school did mention that the school guidance counselors were not used to their graduates going away for college and attending selective colleges. This youth was able to challenge her school counselor to complete all the college admission documentation she needed to gain admission to a competitive school. By doing so, she probably opened the eyes of the school to what is possible for minorities, immigrants, and Black students.

Parental pressure

A central theme across the interviews, as mentioned earlier in this book, was that Nigerian parents are strict and demanding when it comes to education and the expectations they hold about the career choices for their children. A crucial and related issue was the difficult question of whether second-generation should follow their passion or their parents' plan for career and college major. Three youth in the in-depth interview, as well as the focus-group participants, acknowledged there was a parental push for them to go into certain careers and competitive colleges. Nigerian parents steered their children to certain careers such as medicine, law, and engineering. The desire for trophy degrees (professional degrees) and colleges (Ivy League and elite colleges) were attributed to the fact that Nigerians are also "achievement-oriented", as one youth observed. This youth explained part of her motivation as follows: "The Nigerian community focuses on doing well and distinguishing themselves. They refer to what their children are doing because Nigerians are competitive. Every Nigerian parent wants to say they have a daughter or a son who went to such and such a school." I observed that Nigerian parents who experienced a history of underemployment or unemployment in their family tended to push their children into professional degrees where their children can easily secure employment upon graduation. They could have seen fields such as medicine, nursing, pharmacy, and/or engineering as job insurance for their children to help reduce racial discrimination in the job market for their children. It is not uncommon to see Nigerian families with one or two parents who are nurses where all the children are steered toward nursing or other health-care fields. Some second-generation Nigerian youth go from a degree in nursing to medicine. Nursing is deemed as a stepping-stone to the ultimate prized field of medicine in the career hierarchy for Nigerians.

Another youth, who grew up with a physician father and a mother with a law degree, wanted to attend a competitive non-Ivy private university and had received a full scholarship to attend. But when an Ivy League college admission letter came, she said that she knew right away she was going to the Ivy League college. She remembered crying herself to bed because she would have to attend the college her parents wanted if they were willing to pay for the education. But she was appreciative of the sacrifices her parents were making to pay for her college education and was doing her part through work-study and as a resident advisor.

One youth attributed the academic success of high-achieving second-generation Nigerian youth to three factors: Nigerian parents' push for certain careers for their children, parental expectations, and value for education. He also mentioned that second-generation Nigerian youth were taught that education was first. This youth who switched out of pre-med after a difficult first year in college observed that among his Nigerian friends in college, "50% started out as pre-med and now you easily cut that into half. Everyone discovers that you can't force yourself into [medicine]." My findings corroborated this youth's observations. Of the sixteen youth in the study, nine entered college as pre-meds but three eventually earned a medical degree.

He shared that one of the greatest difficulties in his life so far was the decision to change his major from pre-med to explore other career paths, as he did not want to disappoint his parents and well-wishers. He described the difficulty of making the transition to another major as follows: "I remember one of the most wrecking and terrifying moments of my life was when I told them I was going to change my major. I told them [parents] and they saw my face and they said it was okay. It is only when I have no plans and goals that they have a problem with." This youth had found his calling in the social sciences and he said his grades improved dramatically as he was doing what he loved to do. Luckily for him, his parents were supportive of his decision to follow his passion.

The youth who was attending graduate school also indicated that deciding on a college major and a career path had been one of her challenges. She admitted that her parents were uneasy when she switched from pre-med to economics. Her parents remained uneasy until she graduated from college and started and ran her own consulting firm for a year before heading to graduate school at an Ivy League university. She had subsequently proved to her parents that going to medical school was not the only way to earn a good living in the United States or to gain status. Her parents would not have conceived of this career path because they may not have known anyone in that line of business.

The focus-group participants had similar experiences with their parents steering them to certain careers, referring to the previously reported joke that "all Nigerians were pre-med by default." Five members of the focus-group interview described similar experiences in trying to pick a college major. One youth indicated that she really wanted to study sociology and her father discouraged her with, "What are going to do with that?" She eventually negotiated with her father and chose English as a major. The group shared that they hated hearing the apparent question, "What are going to do with that?" Two focus-group participants stated that Nigerian parents were primarily concerned about the ability of their children to make a living in a country they perceive as discriminatory when it comes to Black people and that influenced the career aspirations they set for their children and others concurred. As Black people, their parents understood the challenges of racial discrimination in America and wanted their children to have an edge in the competitive job market. There is research that supports that some minority groups steer their children to certain careers to shield them from discrimination as in the case of Asian-Americans (Sue & Okazaki, 1990). However, the second-generation Nigerian youth that I interviewed also observed that their parents gave them more leeway in terms of their major because parents believed that with an Ivy League degree, they would always do well as opposed to their siblings attending state colleges. The youth who majored in English said that her father rationalized that a degree in English from an Ivy League college is versatile.

An extreme case of parental pressure was revealed by one of the participants in the focus-group who shared a story of an Ivy League student who was estranged from her father and the entire family over her change of college major. As a result, this youth could not go home during the holidays. Another incident that came up with one youth in the in-depth interview was the case of a second-generation Nigerian youth who reportedly committed suicide over parental pressure to achieve in school. This issue requires further exploration and research.

The issue of parental pressure to pursue a certain career path was widespread among Nigerian parents, as it came up in the individual and focus-group interviews. One youth suggested that the role of Nigerian parents in the career paths of second-generation Nigerian youth could be explored further. The oldest youth in the study summarized this problem succinctly when she stated, "I think many Nigerian parents are fixated in careers such as medicine, law, and engineering, and they get uneasy when their children do not go that route." All youth agreed that Nigerian parents place a premium on education as the avenue to a better future and that could be the reason they push their children to do well in school. The parents also grew up in a country where certain careers are glorified because of the respect accrued from such fields.

In Nigeria, everyone yearns for not just a title, but multiple titles and Nigerian parents have transplanted that culture to America. Nigerians display all their academic degrees and titles against their names and the longer such list, the more respect accrued to the holders. So, one might see the following attached to someone's name: MD, PhD, MPH, MBA, Prof., Engr., Arch., Atty. Barr., Dr., JD., PharmD., Ed.D., Chief, etc. Unfortunately, second-generation youth, while they hold their parents' educational attainment and career aspirations, may not aspire for the multitudes of titles their parents have grown accustomed to as they do not see those as a measure of success. I observed that some of the youth wanted the opportunity to help others and aspired to a career in the public sector and were not driven by money or titles. This included those in pre-med. So, for some second-generation Nigerians in the United States, happiness, and personal fulfillment through service to humanity might trump multiple titles, pedigrees, and financial gains or high-status jobs. It will be interesting to see how these perspectives would impact the educational outcomes of future third-generation Nigerians in the United States.

Fear of Racialization of Success

An issue that arose for two youth was the notion that some people saw them as token Blacks that got this far based on their skin color rather than their hard work. They resented their academic achievement being racialized and attributed to race-based programs such as affirmative action. One youth, who was involved in several extra-curricular activities, and had an SAT score of 1450 out of 1600, a GPA of 4.40, and who was in the top 5% of her class, was elated to qualify for the National Merit Scholar Finalist in addition to the National Achievement Scholar—the latter offering recognition for academically talented Black students. As she stated, "This definitely made me equal in the eyes of other students and administrators. I was not just that smart Black girl, or the smartest Black person [in her class]. I was one of the smart kids. I did well enough to be recognized by the regular, mainstream criteria, and not just for the Black award."

She further described how she felt about being racialized: "I applied and got many of the non-need-based Black scholarships in high school. At the senior awards ceremony, I got called to the stage so many times for Black awards and the other regular awards. It was almost embarrassing because some people started saying that I got the scholarships just because I was Black. People said the same about my getting into the Ivy League. Other people from my class who had been ranked higher than me did not get in, and some people said that it was because I was Black. Therefore, there is always at the back of your mind, self-doubt and wondering that, if I weren't Black, would I have gotten in? Even doing as well as I did on PSAT, SAT, and with my 4.40 GPA." Another youth in the focus-group interview talked about being labeled the "token Black" at his part-time job. Although he acknowledged being the token Black in that setting as the only Black, he admitted that he resented all his academic credentials being reduced to race. One focus-group participant summed up her experience with being racialized this way, "In high school, white kids would say that you are not like the other Black kids. You do well and got into [Ivy]. The valedictorian the year before did not get in, so the white kids concluded that I got in because I was Black."

It appeared that high-achieving second-generation Nigerian youth seek recognition based on their accomplishments rather than on their race. Attributing their achievements to their race discounts all their efforts and hard work, creating self-doubt in the youth. It is an additional burden of being Black and high-achieving in a society that devalues Black achievement because of racism.

CHAPTER 9

Coping Strategies of High-Achieving Second-Generation Nigerian Youth in the Study

High-achieving second-generation Nigerian youth face several challenges as they navigated their way to academic excellence. It was not an option for these youth to fail academically, so they devised their unique strategies to navigate the educational terrains and their identities. They coped with the challenges they faced using the following strategies: code-switching, extra-curricular participation, and increased determination and effort.

Code-switching

Code-switching is often viewed from the perspective of linguistics (Delpit, 1988) but for the purpose of this study, it has been broadened to include couture. One youth described the transformation of her high school landscape during her four years as the school became more diverse. To negotiate her identity, academic achievement, and friendship with peers, she used code-switching as a coping strategy. She noted that African-Americans in the regular classes taunted her, although she had African-American friends from her higher-level classes. As a result, she code-witched between African-American vernacular and mainstream speech patterns when interacting with her peers to fit in and to avoid being teased. She also indicated that her code-switching was not limited to speech, as she sometimes code-switched her dressing style. She has continued to do so in college and stated: "I code-switched in speech patterns and dressing sometimes; I definitely dress up more, dress to impress when I know I'm going to something with a lot of Black people, even on this campus [Ivy League college]."

Multiple participants code-switched between African-American vernacular, the use of Nigerian accent, and mainstream speech patterns. When the issue of code-switching came up in the focus-group, one participant stated, "A lot of my friends are Nigerians. I code-switch, especially with Nigerians. We switch codes. When I speak to non-Americans, I try not to sound so Americanized. To Americans, I sound more American, but to others that are not Americans, I try to sound less American." Another focus-group participant added, "I have a little Nigerian accent for fun, especially on the phone. I change my accent often. When I am talking to African-Americans, I sound Black and when I am talking to Asians, I sound more American [standard English]. Even my speed changes depending on whom I am talking to." Another focus-group participant revealed that code-switching was a significant part of her life. She stated, "I am used to it, it has become second nature to me. I do it so much that I do not [even] notice it, but others do. I often switch to my Nigerian accent when I am serious. I had a disagreement with a friend and from the way I spoke, he told me that he knew I was dead serious because I got my Nigerian accent on."

All youth who admitted to code-switching also explained that this practice served an important role in their life. One focus-group participant stated, "We code-switch so we can relate to others. I don't want to sound like I am high and mighty." The same youth also added, "It is just a way to make life easier, not just a Nigerian thing. There is a corporate me, student me, and just me." Another youth noted that her parents were not pleased when she code-switched to African-America vernacular. According to this youth, "My parents say I am talking too Black when I am on the phone with African-American friends. They always say 'why are you talking like that? Do not hang out with African-Americans and they get uneasy when they hear me code-switch to the Black vernacular. And I ask them, why do you speak pidgin, Igbo, Yoruba, and English?"

The youth reminded her parents that when they speak pidgin (the Nigerian version of Ebonics or African-American vernacular), a Nigerian language, or English, they too are code-switching. One youth said, "we code-switch so that relatives can hear and understand you and won't say you are now an American." The youth want to maintain their in-group status and identity through code-switching. They understood that code-switching allowed them to successfully navigate their multidimensional and multicontextual worlds. One focus-group participant said with pride, "When I visit Nigeria, I speak Pidgin English to relatives." One can see that code-switching helped youth effectively navigate their multiple worlds, including helping them to gain acceptance not just amongst their peers but amongst their Nigerian relatives and community, both in the United States and in Nigeria. Their parents may just need a lesson on the benefits of code-switching to catch on. They already practice it but lack self-awareness or the name for it. From my knowledge of Nigerian parents, nothing would please them more than their children being able to relate to relatives by speaking the same language, even with a little accent.

Extra-Curricular Involvements

The level, list, and nature of extra-curricular involvements of the participants in the study were impressive, with many students holding leadership roles in multiple organizations both in school and in their community. All youth in the study reported that they were engaged in several activities, both at the high school and college level. The categories of extra-curriculars included religious, cultural, sports, community-based, and school-based activities, with a variety of motivations behind them. Besides building a resume for college admissions, participation in various extra-curricular activities enabled high-achieving second-generation Nigerian youth to form friendships and bonds with similarly-minded peers as well as some adults. This helped them to create social networks necessary for academic success and future social capital beyond college. Evidently, extra-curricular involvement served as a coping mechanism for the youth as it helped them to occupy themselves productively while creating social bonds and networks. The youth and their parents understood that they need more than good grades, high grade point averages, high class rank and high standardized test scores to gain admission to America's top colleges. Parents also believed in keeping their children busy to avoid the "devil's workshop," as my mother would often say. They realized their children were less likely to get in trouble if they were actively engaged in constructive activities. The youth also explored and found their niche in activities that they felt passionate about.

Five youth indicated that extra-curricular activities took a lot of their time, but that they needed those activities to save their sanity and to create a balance between their academic and social lives. One high school youth indicated that his parents encouraged him to participate in extra-curricular activities in preparation for college. Another youth reported participation in high school orchestra as a violin player. Their parents allowed them to explore their interests. Two youth said they had to find employment after the age of sixteen for financial help with their expenses.

Several youth participants had enough extra-curriculars to fill up their non-school schedules. For example, one high school student noted, "I hardly have any time after school because of activities. When I come home, I am so tired that I sit for a while, eat, sleep a little before I do my homework whether it takes me to 1:00 am and sometimes more. It does [it does take me that long] because my activities back me up. I must sleep before I start the homework." He also reported being active in track, stage, multicultural club, poetry club, and literary magazine, and model United Nations. Many others shared the same experience with regards to the number of their extra-curricular involvement.

All the youth reported that homework was a priority in their family and must be done when they got home before anything else. Whether the youth did homework immediately after getting home or later, it was built into their daily routines and they did not need any reminder for their homework to be done. Five youth reported holding leadership positions in clubs. For example, one described his extra-curricular involvement in high school as follows: "After school, depending on the day, as I had different activities every day, I was a superman. If I were in a club, I was the vice president or president. I was in prom committee, student council, captain of the volleyball team, and president of Junior Achievement."

The oldest youth started her day with an extra-curricular activity. Describing her involvement as follows: "My day started early, especially as I was involved in student government, which met early before the school day. I went to classes and played tennis after classes during season from 3 to 7 or 8 pm. After tennis, I studied typically from 8-12 midnight or 1:00 AM depending. Tennis was a daily activity, and I did other extra-curricular activities. I was heavily involved in extra-curricular activities or clubs from career to tennis and community services. Weekends were devoted entirely to homework."

Another youth also reported that her days were long due to her extra-curricular activities. She stated, "I stayed in school for extra-curricular activities. I was a member of the student council, prom committee, Just K [a Christian youth group], Building-With-Books [a community service organization], and Junior Achievement. I was the vice-president of finance for one year. I was involved in school and I usually didn't see home until late because of the activities."

Another youth stated that she was also actively involved in the school. "I belonged to several clubs. I was in the African-American club for three years and I was a vice president and president of the club. I was in Interact Club, which is a community service club. I was in the National Honor Society. I was a member of the State Board of Education." Some youth participated in activities that helped with college preparation, such as the club that took local urban high school kids on college tours to get an early preview of college life.

All youth reportedly volunteered in the community in addition to their other activities. For some youth who attended parochial high schools, volunteering in the community was a requirement for graduation. One youth who started volunteering as a requirement for a class, ended up volunteering in a daycare, elderly home, and a homeless shelter, in addition to tutoring elementary school kids while she was in high school. Another youth, who attended the same high school relayed a similar experience "A major activity on my résumé is Sunday school teaching. First, I started as an aide and became a teacher for 4 years until I graduated. I was part of Building-With-Books, and we did a fundraiser to send kids to Third World countries to build schools. I was in the chorus and I am still doing it in college. I like choir because it brings me back to reality and it is my most rewarding activity. I was a member of the prom council for two years. At school, we were required to put in some hours in a year volunteering, but I ended up volunteering all year." On Fridays, when she did not have much extra-curricular activity in school, she also volunteered to help in the office. Nine youth were involved in church activities in addition to other activities. One was a member of the youth church group and a choir member; another was a part of the youth community of her church in addition to her membership in the National Honor Society, Spanish Honor Society, color guard, yearbook, and creative writing club, as well as her tutoring of younger students in chemistry and math.

One participant was a member of the National Honor Society, National Society of Black Engineers (NSBE), and Smart Start, a youth group of her church for which she served as the secretary. She was also a member of Usher's Guild and the vice president of NSBE. When asked why she participated in extra-curricular activities, the oldest student participant in the study responded: "In high school, I know how the system worked to get into college. I played tennis because I liked it and for the exercise. I am not into sports for activities. It was the pressure to get into college. But in college, I did less because I did not have the pressure to do it. So once the pressure was lifted, I did not do as much. I didn't play sports in college and I didn't play in graduate school." A high school student also indicated that his parents encouraged him to participate in extra-curricular activities because it would help him to get into a college. He also said that he participated in extra-curricular activities because of the benefits of meeting different people.

Unlike the oldest participant, who reduced her extra-curricular activity in college, one Ivy League college participant continued her activities. She stated, "I am involved in many extra-curricular activities. Residential College Advisor (RA), Eating Concerns Peer Educator, African dance troupe, Club Volleyball, Co-chair of Community House [community Service Organization], and a board member of a non-profit group. I run the Sib Program, which served minority youth in grades 7 and 8 in the community, Christian Fellowship member, Minority Association of pre-med, Black Students Union Leadership and Mentoring Program, and I also work in a neuroscience lab for independent study in addition to a work-study job." She understood that extra-curricular involvement in college cut her study time, but she saw the value in these forms of participation. She described her reasons: "They provided the opportunity because different groups wanted me to do different things. For example, the African-American Awareness Club gave me leadership positions, responsibility, and the chance to show others that I am responsible. Volleyball was discipline-oriented and traditionally our team has won the state championship 14 out of the past 17 years or so. Working with teammates help to mold me to learn teamwork and adjust to those around me. Track helps me to challenge myself as an individual and push myself beyond my limits. In college, I continued what I did in high school, minus track, but more activities. College is more involved, and I am learning to help others help themselves. Christian Fellowship is for personal spiritual growth. RA is interesting because it helps me to help people with their daily things. You need good judgment because people are looking up to you in ability to resolve conflicts in a fair manner. You also need to have the ability to manage emergency situations while keeping calm. All of these things help mold me into a mature person." Another youth, a high school senior, added that "community service instills something in you. It also humbles you. You build your character by helping others and that helps you. You get to know people you will never get to know to talk to you. You meet people with the same drive and see people from different groups interact."

Yet in college, four students reduced the level of their extra-curricular activities and selected activities that were more enjoyable to them. For example, one indicated that she reduced the number of activities she participated in college after her first year to devote more time to her studies, but she was heavily recruited to stay on in some associations. She stated, "In college, I was a member of Nigerian Students Association. The Association recruited me, and I was the freshman reporter. I am a member of the Black Women's Support Network. The groups sought me out and voted me the president for the next year. I am also involved in other foundations. The activities keep me busy. I spend three hours a week in the choir during the weekend and during concert season, there are daily rehearsals, but it is extremely rewarding." Two siblings who attended the same parochial high school also indicated they reduced their extra-curricular participation in college. This might have been tied to their previously stated need to devote more time to their studies due to their high school's lack of adequate preparation.

However, their older sibling noted, "In college, I am part of the Sorority Sigma Delta, National Society of Black Engineers, Nigerian Students Association, and an Executive Board Member of our Lifestyle Magazine, Board Member of Coalition for the Pan African Scholars." Although she faced the same challenges of under-preparedness for the rigors of an Ivy League college, she strategically continued to participate and juggle her academics and many extra-curricular activities in college and one of her siblings had mentioned that she cultivated effective study skills in high school. This could have helped her to manage all her activities in college.

Increased Determination and Effort

Two youth admitted to having experienced academic difficulty on the survey. Yet eight participants talked about academic difficulty during the interview. I would have expected the reverse because the surveys were more impersonal. The four-college youth who attended the same urban parochial school indicated that the high school did not adequately prepare them for the academic rigors of highly selective colleges. Another college youth, who attended a suburban public high school, had trouble in organic chemistry. All the college youth admitted to working harder due to the competitive nature of the colleges they attended. One high school student who attended an urban public school prior to his current suburban public school admitted that he too was ill-prepared for the academic rigors of his suburban high school. Two other high school youth talked about the challenges of taking rigorous courses and how they persevered.

Although the study participants were academic achievers as their history previously demonstrated, some of them encountered difficulties due to the academic rigors of their classes. As a result, the youth reassessed their needs and found solutions to their difficulties on their own or by reaching out to others. They changed their strategies and increased their efforts and determination. They sought help from teachers, parents, and peers (through study groups), and increased their efforts by developing a study habit.

One youth attending an Ivy League college from an urban parochial high school admitted to lacking study skills in high school and had to develop one in college after facing academic challenges. One of his siblings, who is also attending the same Ivy League college and graduated as her high school valedictorian, described how she coped with her challenges as follows: "I sat back and reevaluated, figuring out what is not working and finding out what works. It was a mindset thing. I came to this [college] thinking that I did well in high school so it will be easy. I had to change my method and I reevaluated my strategies." She realized that she could not be the valedictorian at the Ivy League and redefined her priorities according to reality.

The fact that high-achieving second-generation Nigerian youth performed well in high school made it more difficult for one youth to accept that he was having academic difficulty. Relating his experiences about his first year in college, he noted: "The biggest problem was admitting that I had a difficulty. If I spoke earlier, it would have been helped. If you were known to be smart, you do not want to admit that you have academic difficulty. I went to study sessions, talked to the teaching assistants, and professors." He learned to humble himself and sought academic help. His older sibling told a similar story: "Well, basically due to the lack of preparation in high school, my first semester was a shock and my grades reflected that. I had to learn how to study and study well because I did not learn it in high school. I had to learn to be okay with doing my best. I had to struggle with that because our whole lives, straight-A defined success. I had to identify what true success is. It is not just grade point average but my sanity, being able to sleep and eat. I had to redefine success. Success is not just black and white or one size fits all." She needed to re-evaluate what her definition of academic success meant. The focus-group youth also shared the opinion that being on an Ivy League campus made them re-evaluate what it meant to be successful. Admission to an elite college is already a success. The greater success is now to graduate without losing their sanity.

For two youth, the solution to academic challenges was hiring a private tutor. One of them who also was an Ivy League student and planning to attend medical school, decided to hire a tutor for her organic chemistry class, which she said she hated and in which she earned the only C grade of her life. Likewise, another youth who was attending a competitive private college said: "Everything seemed different in college and I couldn't do the same things I did in high school in college. The competition was greater in college, so I had to change or get the same results." Her strategy was different as she acknowledged that she sought out study groups and made other changes. She described the changes she made as follows: "For the physiology, I was overwhelmed because I was a freshman, so I joined a study group and got a tutor. For biology, it was difficult because it was not a class I was fond of and I lacked focus. For anatomy, I had to change my study habits because the course was different from any other class I had ever taken." She also indicated that the lesson she learned from the experience was that "hard work and interest work." She concluded that she would not have done well in those classes if she were not genuinely interested in her major. This could have prompted her to speculate about the effects of second-generation Nigerian youth being pushed into areas they were not interested in and to her suggestion for that topic as a possible follow-up study. She believes that youth would do better in courses they are interested in. She was keenly aware of such pressure as she was majoring in psychology and nursing at the urging of her parents because to her parents, a psychology degree may not earn her a job in the future. Apparently, the nursing major was job insurance even though she appeared to have little inclinations to pursue nursing.

For the high school youth, their strategies revolved around getting help from teachers and parents and studying more. One high school sophomore explained that he was having difficulty in chemistry and went to the teacher for extra help. The teacher helped him and explained how he could do better in the class and made him comfortable in the class. He had considered dropping the class and his parents urged him not to. So, with parental support and teacher support, he completed chemistry Honors class with a B. This was significant as it showed that parental support and teacher support could offset potential academic failures of students. For two siblings who were also in high school, they increased their efforts in studying and got help in math homework from their father, who was a college professor. For these youth, all that was needed to cope with an academic challenge was the ability to seek and receive help from others. They learned to adjust and take the necessary steps needed to do well in school.

CHAPTER 10

Parents' Voices

High-achieving second-generation Nigerian youth in the in-depth interview group shared some similar characteristics in their family backgrounds. They grew up in two-parent homes and their parents were college graduates, many with graduate or professional degrees. Most of the parents were gainfully employed and were in the middle or upper-middle-class income strata. Survey data indicated their parents came to the United States to further their education and most of them received their college education in the United States. Four youth grew up in a suburb, while seven of them lived in an urban setting.

The focus-group interview participants shared similar family backgrounds as the in-depth individual interview group. Parents of the focus-group were also college graduates but had more professional and graduate degrees than their counterparts in the individual interview group. All focus-group participants also grew up in a two-parent household and their parents also came to the United States to further their education.

Fathers of the focus-group participants had professional degrees and professional jobs. A disparate number of their mothers had professional degrees compared to the individual in-depth interview participants, and all mothers of the focus-group participants had traditional professional jobs, except for one who was self-employed. Like the in-depth interview participants, parents of the focus-group participants were in the middle or upper-middle-class income strata. While two focus-group participants grew up in an urban setting, four of them grew up in a suburb. A greater number of the focus-group participants grew up in the suburb in comparison to the individual in-depth interview group.

Survey data showed that most of the parents (mothers) interviewed obtained their college education in the United States. During the interview of the mothers, they indicated that they came to the United States to join their husbands who were pursuing an education here. This supported survey data completed by the youth. One mother was in the United States on a Nigerian government-sponsored scholarship, pursuing her education when she met her husband who was also a student. All parent participants had lived in the United States for at least ten years as of 2007. One parent had resided in the United States for over three decades at the time of the interview.

All mothers who participated in the interview had a college degree and had professional jobs, except for one mother who was home with her children. During her interview, she indicated that she was enrolled in a master's degree program with the anticipation of securing employment. She came to the United States with a bachelor's degree from the United Kingdom, revealing during the interview that it was difficult to secure employment in the United States with a degree from a foreign country. After attempting to gain employment, her husband told her to stay home with their children.

The educational attainment levels of the Nigerian parents in the sample support what researchers have found about Nigerian immigrants in the United States which is that Nigerian immigrants are among the most educated group in the United States (Butcher, 1994; Massey et al. 2007). Educated or not, the voices of parents of color are often absent in the discourse about the academic experiences of their children (Auerbach, 2002) and omitted in educational research (Delgado-Gaitan, 1991; Delpit, 1988; Meyers et al., 2000; Fine, 1993; Villenas & Deyhle, 1999). I included the parents' voices here so that readers can see how parents' experiences and beliefs could have influenced the youths' perceptions and beliefs about their academic achievements and to determine whether the parents' views closely align or differ from the second-generation Nigerian youth that participated in the study. I asked all the mothers the same questions and pursued follow-up questions when needed.

What type of experiences have you had living in the United States?

Parent A: "First, I learned that England is more conservative than here and that it is easier to get a job here than in the U.K., especially if you were educated here. There is also less discrimination here than in England." This came from the mother who was unable to secure employment with her degree from the U.K. and has enrolled in graduate school while raising her children. Her response could be because her husband was able to secure teaching at a university after they arrived in the United States.

Parent B: "I had some challenges that I had to overcome. With school, it was in choosing what I wanted to do. There was discouragement from school officials, starting from the secretary saying, 'Why don't you do a 2-year program instead of a 4-year program, do you think that you can do it'? I still remember that day like today. Maybe because of the program I entered [nursing]. Thinking back, I found out why she said it might be because during that time, I was having babies and going to school. After I finished the nursing program, there was a freeze in employment right after I finished. The only group hiring was the nursing homes and mostly when you finish a nursing program; you want to work in a hospital to gain more experience. In the nursing home, it looks like you do the same things every day. That is why most nurses do not want to work in the nursing homes even though they pay more than the hospitals. When I finally started working in a hospital, there was a pinning ceremony for new nurses where you get a pin with your qualifications and where you received your training. I wore my pin to work in a 2nd floor of this hospital not knowing that the head nurse in my unit was not a BSN graduate. Well, they gave me hell there and I overheard the head nurse through a nursing assistant asking who that Black nurse with an accent was. They would not even show me what they were doing. It was an ugly experience. Because I had kids, I wanted a suitable shift (3-11 PM) so that I could get my kids to school but this woman constantly assigned me the morning shift where I had to leave the house at 6-6:15 AM to avoid the traffic and be at work at 7:00 AM. So, my kids had a rough time as a result. After three weeks, I called my director and told her that I was not coming back because I was being stressed out. So, the second job I did, as I usually have a full time and a part-time job became my full-time job. The director was one of my instructors in college and I was there for 13 years as a supervisor."

Interviewer to Parent B: And what is the difference between a 2-year program and a 4-year program?

Parent B: "For me, it meant repeating what I did back home. It was the Associate Degree that I did at home. The difference is academics."

Parent C: "I really learnt a lot in this country. Even though I was an adult when I came here, I learnt a lot because of my background. I was able to cope, able to have my education, have three kids, and have my [multiple] houses, work and keep my job for almost ten years since I finished college. I have been able to take care of my children, telling them that education is important, and they see it and follow in my footsteps. I never have any bad comments about America besides the racism. My personality is that I can cope. I can communicate with my coworkers. Sometimes I come home, and my kids drive me crazy and sometimes they are ok, and I am giving them a hard time, but they know that it is for their good."

Parent D: "Because we came here by choice to further our education, we had basic college education from home. Both my husband and I went to Teachers College and my husband came here to get an American education. His parents paid for him as a private student to come here and study and he came on an F1 student visa. He felt that I can also get my own education and I joined him on an F2 visa. Having gained much from our parents, we knew we had to concentrate on our education and that we had to know and do one thing at a time, but I personally had to do two things at a time. I came to the U.S. pregnant and I had to be a mother and my husband insisted that I start school. He wanted me to study and not work and he knew that I could do it in record time. I did not have to work, and I finished in record time. He was willing to pay for me to get an education because his dad cannot pay for his wife. My first degree was hard and so I had to go for science education because it was getting hard for my husband and I gave up my pharmacy program. As I look back, my father was a retired school principal, and my mother-in-law was a retired school headmistress. So, on both sides, education was major. We [in our family] have been raising people and training people. I am not the type to sit behind a counter. After I looked at myself, I know that [teaching] is where I belong. God blessed me with children, and I think God placed me there [teaching job] to raise my children. Being in the public school has helped and motivated me to learn how the educational system works here. Teaching helped [me] to be able to do my job as a parent. I will be able to get home and do dinner for the family. I graduated with my fourth child. I was the last to march on the line with a week-old baby and it was made a joke of at the graduation that I graduated with honors. Mothers are naturally the first teachers for their children. So, there are many advantages to being a teacher and that took me to become a teacher. I had inside advantages being in the public school. The beginning of a youth is a fear of God. We know we were Roman Catholics and Christians. In Nigeria, education is the moral base, and being in the public school here, there was not any continuity. What we had in Nigeria was not available here. We started seeing the differences. Our daughter was the first one to experience the public school and she came home in first grade and was so disappointed about how the students did not have any respect for the teachers and the bathrooms were very dirty. She complained about the school and said she hoped that she was not going back there. I was in secondary education and had no idea of what the public elementary schools looked like. But we moved to another area and the first thing we did was to find a church and we registered. We found out that there were many advantages to being a parishioner. We applied to the school for my daughter, but we were waitlisted. The next spring, she was accepted to a Catholic school. From there we learned so much. We really did not have any plans. So, from then, the next ones went to the same school, but it was not easy because of the tuition. I did not continue with my education. From 1991, I got my first job as a per diem teacher to help my husband who was self-employed, and I started [a program for Nigerian children] and there were two incomes coming into the family. We concentrated on paying the tuition. By 1991, when my daughter was in the first grade, we bought our first home in the same area. The older children attended [parochial] school. Our motivation for sending them to a Catholic school is the discipline and the learning in terms of keeping things clean, listening to teachers, and they all contribute to the moral upbringing. We felt that we were Catholics and our parents invested in us and our children should be exposed to Catholic education. The Catholic school provided all that to my children. My children do not waste anything because of the way they grew up. We were not sending money to Nigeria because our parents expected us to take care of ourselves because of the nature of our families. So, we invested our money on the education of our children." This family is unlike many Nigerian immigrants where parents make similar sacrifices to educate their children while supporting multitudes of family members in Nigeria.

Parent E: "Well, I will say that my experiences in the United States had been a mixed bag. There had been a lot of highs and lows. Education-wise, things proceeded well because I was able to go straight through my education, but I hit some roadblocks because of economic and family problems. Family wise, I was not able to find work and a lot of things converged to create economic difficulties interfering with my being able to raise my children properly and to attend to my studies. So, like I said, it was a mixed bag, some good years and some bad years."

Parent F: "In general, I would say in the differences in culture between our background and here and trying to blend it together in terms of going to school and raising the children. It was always something that we had to battle. It is something that stood out between living here and raising the kids here." This mother was referring to how Nigerian immigrants in the United States experience cultural differences as they struggle to raise their children while juggling multiple roles.

What does success mean to you?

Parent A: "Once you have Christ, when you have that, you are rich in everything. It is the spirit of God that guides you, even in education. Education is another way to the top because without education one is nothing." This speaks to the reverence Nigerians have for education.

Parent B: "Success depends on how you look at things. In terms of education and career, success to me is always being able to get a job. Success is to be able to stand on your own, to become independent. Of course, my kids know that our utmost goal is to be sure that they all get a good education, which is the direction all of them are going."

Parent C: "Success means a lot to me. That is why I was able to pull myself up in life the way it is now. It makes me happy and gives me rest of mind. Success is education, family, and it is like planting a tree and seeing it grow in a normal way without losing the leaves. Success is all the accomplishment, seeing my children moving up, seeing myself imparting the knowledge I got to my children, and using the knowledge the right way."

Parent D: "Success to me is having expectations for myself and if I see myself accomplishing those goals then I am successful. When I came to the U.S. I believed that I would have a degree higher than [what] I had when I arrived, and I achieved it. Being a mother was hard and I achieved it. In the family area, I married the person I loved, and I had no regrets. I have fulfilled my own part as a mother and that's success to me. I set goals for my children and I see them following the goals."

Parent E: "Success to me is being happy. This is because happiness means that I have met some goals I set for myself. Sometimes, I look back and I am happy, and it is because I have met some goals, I set for myself. The goal could be helping others, myself, or finishing a project. Success is defined in the affective. It is the feeling and the confidence to say I did it. I equate success with happiness."

Parent F: "Success to me is what you have achieved as a parent, and as an individual in a society. It is not wealth accumulation but how well you have established yourself in society and raised your children in society."

Do you consider yourself an academic success?

Parent A: "Yes, I do because it is the only way. If I did not have a degree in Finance, I will not be able to do what I am doing now" (The interviewee was a stay-at-home mother of four, who was then pursuing a graduate degree). She added: "Without the education I had, I will not have a goal. My goal is a better future, a better job, and to earn myself a better living."

Parent B: "Yes, I consider myself academically successful in a way because I was able to finish my education even with all those odds against me. Even though I intended to read further but due to family circumstances, I couldn't continue with that because we decided to focus on the kids."

Parent C: Yes, because I was able to go through what I went through, have three children, and get at least a B.S Degree and I have not stopped. Even though the kids are in school, I am thinking about going back to school in a short while."

Parent E: "Yes, while I was in school, I did very well. I feel that I did not really accomplish the goal that I set for myself in terms of getting the PhD. But I have dealt with it pragmatically. I am a pragmatic person. I have a pragmatic side. People tell me that I am very smart.

I work hard and I know I can do it. I believe that I am successful [at self-efficacy and optimism]."

Parent F: "Yes I consider myself a success academically because of the fact that the basic education I have received from elementary school to high school and college and being in the professional world and using that education in my job as an accountant."

Do you consider your children academically successful?

Parent A: "Yes, I do because they are really doing well in their education, are honor and A students, follow the steps of their parents and they know the value of the education they are receiving."

Parent B: "Yes, because most have gotten their college education."

Parent C: "Yes of course! They have never been [held back in school]. I am always getting compliments from their teachers and peers. I am enormously proud of them and myself and my husband pray that they will continue, and they have not disappointed us yet. For now, God is great."

Parent D: "Yes, I consider my children successful. They listen, apply themselves and I have high standards. When I look around my house, I find my children successful. Being in public school, I look at how things are, and I can say my children are remarkable. There are differences in [ranking of] schools. I went to a state college and I did not know the differences before but at work, I learned from colleagues who live in the suburbs that schools are rated in the State. I learned about the five highly rated schools and I was exposed to colleagues who were born here, and I found out how society is. So, my goal became to send my children to the best schools there are. To get into the best colleges in the state, kids need to graduate from the best Catholic high schools or the special schools, and they must work hard. My children were in Catholic schools where there was stiff competition and where academics are the most important thing, not just attendance. The special schools and Catholic schools were the only ones we considered for our children. So, I got to know that for my children, academic merit gets them to the best schools. I learned that the least ranked special school was better than the best public school. So, we started preparing the kids. If they got a full scholarship to a Catholic school, it was better than the special schools. My daughter was accepted into four Catholic schools and they were all fighting for her. Her brother got admission to a special high school, but he got a 75% scholarship to attend the Catholic high school. He went to the Catholic school because the public-school factor was there at the special school. We chose the Catholic school, but we had to move [out of state] because of a family situation and we lost all the scholarships. We came here after the school year has started and the school already gave out all the scholarships and we did not know anybody here. We had already bought a house and we were supposed to close earlier. We drove around the city asking for any Catholic church. We drove into [the parish] and asked the priest we saw whether they have a school here for our five oldest ones. We focused on the older ones and the woman at the school there admitted all of them."

Parent E: "Yes, they are successful academically. I must make one point for them and for me. I know that I could have done more, and I feel that way for them. I know that with their potential, they could have done more. Even for myself, I feel that way. In school, they got good grades, the teachers spoke well of them in report cards, and the principals knew them, and they had leadership roles. These are the markers of academic success, good grades, and the teachers and administrators knowing the students. I also did fundraiser activities for the schools. I met a lot of the teachers and they told me wonderful things about my children and praised them. When they worked, they had strong references from their employers. They came across as responsible wherever they worked."

Parent F: "Yes, my children are successful academically. Even though they are still in school they are doing what they are supposed to be doing at this age. My oldest one is in law school, my second one is in college and my youngest one just finished high school and is in the university world."

What role did you play in making that happen?

Parent A: "I supported them in their homework. In the beginning of each year, I tried to know their teachers and relate with the teachers to let them know that I am one of the student's mothers. I get some of the syllabus—what my children will be learning and help my kids before they go back to school. I make my children understand the meaning of time management in life and to understand that one can never waste his or her time and make effective use of time."

Parent B: "This is my quote to my children. I am your parent; we are here to support you and your job is to study. We are not asking you to pay us money, your job is to go to school, listen to the teachers, come home, and do your homework. You are going to school for you, not for me. That homework is too hard does not count. One thing that helped is that my kids studied together and helped each other as soon as they got back from school."

Parent C: "From kindergarten until my children finished primary school and going to high school, I was active in the PTA, and I was involved in activities in their school. I sneaked into their classrooms and checked with their teachers to make sure that they were doing what they were supposed to do. I also checked in with the principals. I was reading to my children when they were young. They were able to read before they started kindergarten. I still help them with the small knowledge I got. I still discuss their education with them."

Interviewer to Parent C: What type of discussions do you have with them?

Parent C: "When I discuss school with them, I ask them if they have any homework or if they have any question that I can help them with. If they are writing, I ask them if they need my input and I give them my input."

Parent D: "We have a habit of attending all types of meetings and helping in the Parent-Teacher-Association as much as possible. We also contacted teachers. We made it a duty that they line up their homework on the dining table and my husband and I would check all of them one by one. We encouraged them to look at their vision and where they are going as they grew up. We took them to open houses and made decisions for them, as they got older. We learnt that they have more chances as minorities at the Ivy League schools and that these schools depend on the academics not income and so we made up our mind that they should apply to only the Ivy League colleges. All the kids know that they had to do well, participate in school and outside activities, involve themselves in leadership activities. We made sure that they participated fully in all they can do and to know themselves [identity] through the program that I established, the Igbo program. If you do not know who you are, where are you going? I made sure that they participated in the Igbo program. I made sure to let them know where the needs are for minorities in the sciences even if they scored low on the SAT, if they apply to study an area where minorities are underrepresented, they will have a good chance of getting in. We pushed them to write the scholarship applications. We told them that the more you apply for, the better your chances of getting called. We also did not focus on getting money while in high school, so we did not allow them to work. We made sure that they do not love money as kids but to focus on their education. They had to live on whatever their parent gave them. I did not believe in having money to buy whatever you want. As kids, their job is their education."

Parent E: "I would say two things. I was very vocal about my expectations of them. I pointed out myself and family [as models of success]. I made sure that they know the family I came from has high standards and they saw me [working hard]. I made sure that they saw the rewards of academic success.

Interviewer to Parent E: What did you say to them?

Parent E: "Sometimes I would point out to them that certain jobs and positions would get you far. I told them about the value and the ability to move up and make decisions and not be subject to others pushing you around. Because they are girls, it was important to me that they do not depend on a husband. I wanted them to believe that they can take care of themselves and to be independent and happy. I know from Nigeria and here what divorce does to women, and they fall into the poverty line. So, they should not depend on men. Some of this came from stuff happening in the family. It did not make for a happy home. That made them also more determined to succeed for themselves."

Parent F: "As a parent, I would say making sure the kids are successful comes from the background we have. We were brought up knowing that education is the key to success in life. If someone can afford to send you to school, then you must go to school and study. It is what my parents instilled in me as a young person that I try to give to my children in trying to make them successful."

How do you identify yourself?

Parent A: "I am Black African. I am from Nigeria and a native of Yoruba."

Parent B: "I am a Nigerian."

Parent C: "I identify myself as a Nigerian and a typical Igbo woman from Africa. I am proud of where I came from. Some people might think that you are Jamaican or Haitian but no."

Parent D: "If there is a provision, I will write 'other' and put in Igbo-Nigerian. Many other times, I will put Black where the choices are limited to black and white because I am Black but mostly Igbo-Nigerian. I am Black African."

Parent E: "I tell people I am Igbo and Nigerian. It depends on the situation. It often comes up about my accent and people ask and I say I am Igbo. It is rare to come across a time when I identify as African-American except on government forms or paperwork."

Parent F: "I am a Nigerian woman, of the Black race and an American by naturalization."

How do your children identify themselves?

Parent A: "I make them understand that they are from Africa. Some of my children were born in England and are confused about where they are from, but I try to make them believe that they are flesh of Africa" Two of this interviewee's children were born in the U.K. and two were born in the U.S.

Parent B: "They call themselves Nigerian-Americans."

Parent C: "They see themselves as both Nigerians and Americans, but they display more Nigerian attitudes. They copy more from the Nigerian community around them. Their attitude is more of from where their parents came from and they are happy to be part of the Nigerian community even though they feel sometimes we don't practice what we preach."

Interviewer to Parent C: What do you mean by "not practicing what we preach?"

Parent C: "They feel that some Nigerians, their attitudes are fake. They do not show their kids the right behaviors they are expecting from them." I did not pursue this response with the parent but understood from her child that this was about relationships between Nigerian parents that can suffer from conflicts.

Parent D: "I am not so sure."

Parent E: "I believe they really do think of themselves as Nigerians. My oldest one has vocalized and appreciated having been born in Nigeria and raised in the U.S. [she came in at the age of six, not part of the study]. In graduate school, she made a comment about how happy she was about it. My children think of themselves as Nigerians first because even the two younger ones who were born here think of themselves as Nigerians."

Parent F: "That is something that I am still struggling with. They see themselves as partly Americans and partly Nigerians. They know that they are of the Black race, but they do not believe in Black-American. They are Americans just as anybody else."

Interviewer to Parent F: Any idea why that was the case?

Parent F: "I think it is because of the racial issues that have been out there. When they were little, I remember telling them not to let anybody put a stigma on them. I did not want anybody to label them, so it is partly coming from parents because of the stigma put on Black-Americans. Yes, we are Black, and Nigerian and we need to stand for ourselves and believe in what we are."

How do you want your children to identify themselves?

Parent A: "Black African because of the culture and because I don't want them to throw away their culture. Because their parents came from Africa, I want them to belong and not feel like strangers in Africa and to know their ancestors. No matter that their color is Black, even, if they came from England or the U.S, they originated from somewhere."

Parent B: "It would have been my wish that they see themselves as Nigerians—particularly as Igbo and when they are getting married to marry from our town [native town in Nigeria] but it is not working that way."

Parent C: "I am okay with the way they identify themselves [as Nigerian-Americans] as long as they are not displaying a different attitude from what they are learning at home."

Parent D: "I want them to identify themselves as Nigerian-Americans because where we are, everybody is hyphenated. We are Nigerian-Americans just as the Irish-Americans. So, we must stand up to be counted. Although when I hear them talk, they identify as Nigerians." It is interesting to hear some of the parents were more assimilated than their children with their preference for American hyphenated identity.

Parent E: "The way they identify is not a problem for me. I believe that identity is flexible and situational. Today I could be Nigerian, tomorrow Igbo, and the next day African-American. I look at it pragmatically. Depending on where you are, you can pick and use which one works. Technically, I am Black, Igbo, and African-American, so it does not bother me which identity I take, and they can also do the same. They can pick and choose also."

Parent F: "As they are comfortable identifying themselves. Be it Nigerian or Americans but I still don't believe in putting a label on somebody."

What steps and rules did you implement to get your children to focus on academics?

Parent A: "The first rule is that when they come back from school, I check their work, and then they do their homework before they do any other thing."

Parent B: "As a matter of fact, we never set any schedule for them any time. They know what was expected of them. They came home and gathered around the table and did their homework. The way we planned it, I worked the 3-11 pm shift and as soon as they came home, I would leave as they were eating. Soon after that, my husband will return and if they had a problem with their homework, he would help them. Because the older ones started it, the younger ones followed. It became the norm for the family."

Parent C: "I had some rules when they were younger. Before 8:00 pm, homework was done, and they had to go to bed early and get up early, especially when I was in school. That helped me to study when they were younger. That is different now. I always provided them with a structure."

Parent D: "They just have to do all the homework above and beyond. When they were growing up, they were only allowed to watch TV on the weekends. During the week when they finished their homework, they read. They could not isolate or lock themselves up to watch TV. The older ones were self-motivated. The younger ones that I am raising when I am old would argue with me and twist my head. My nine-year-old son asked me why he had to read more than the teacher assigned for homework. So, I went to the teacher and said to her to tell the kids that the assigned reading is the minimum. My younger ones, they get reinforcement in reading and math at home. I have mama's homework, where I will mark out assignments to be done in the major areas of Math and English. We were doing this up until last year, but we have not started it this year. I go out and buy books for them and when they finish their homework, they had to read a book they picked. I am always encouraging them to read more than the 20 minutes the teacher assigned them to read."

Parent E: "I had rules when they were younger. There were homework and assignment time. I made sure to know what they had for homework. They also know that I must know what they had for homework. I asked them and they will tell me. Their life at home was structured. Chores and homework were done. I had a structure for them. I also kept a cane nearby. It was more of a threat for them to know that there is something else I could do."

Parent F: "When they were young, I remember we had a rule on no TV during the week from Sunday to Thursday night because they need to focus on their study, homework, sports activities, and extra events at the school. During the weekends were not a problem and they could stay up to watch TV if you can get up in the morning to do your chores. That was one thing that really helped the children to focus rather than watch TV. They didn't like it and they complained that their friends watched TV during the week, but we said no because they needed to focus."

Do you think that such measures yielded positive results?

Parent A: "I believe that these measures helped. One thing that helped is that from 6th grade, I always get them an organizer to jut down what the teacher said in class and that made them pay attention in class because they know I was going to ask them about what the teacher said."

Parent B: "Yes, I think these measures helped because I didn't see any failure in my children, and I didn't have any need for any adjustments in terms of their study habits. These measures made them to have a good study habit and they focused on their study and success in school."

Parent C: "Yes, I think these measures were helpful. One of the rules I had was that they could not watch TV during the weekdays when they were in grades K-8th. That helped them a lot. Every report card they brought home had mostly A and the teachers never complained about their homework and my children never had any problem with the teachers or the principals."

Parent D: "So far, I think they have been positive. My little boy was trying to get his little sister to go against the rule and not complying. After trying, he realized that he did not have a choice, so he had to do it (i.e., comply with the rules). I did not want to give him too much choice. I do not give them space to be lazy. He went and tried reading and felt happy. So, I know the measure works when he asks me to extend his bedtime so that he can finish reading his book. That tells me that he is enjoying it. The girl also likes it [reading]."

Parent E: "Having a routine for them helped. It was how we lived. The oldest ones who were born in Nigeria had earlier lagged when they arrived and were tested six months later. I made sure that they caught up. Sibling rivalry helped because they wanted to do well, and they competed amongst themselves. They also wanted to please me, and I rewarded them when they did well. They also liked school. They had a social network and they had friends who came to their birthday parties. It was not as if I had to chase them out every morning. They wanted to go to school and they liked going."

Parent F: "Yes, I think that they were helpful to them."

Interviewer to Parent F: What would be an evidence to support that your rules about no TV during the weekday were effective?

Parent F: "I can't conclude that no TV rule worked. I know it helped and I can see that children are different. We have three of them and some you do not need to watch but one you need to watch. Two of my children never had any homework problem and the other one I got calls about him all the time. We did set the rule that after school was snack, nap if needed, and homework but you cannot do homework past 9:00 pm except for if you had a band practice or game. There was a rule that 9:30 pm was bedtime and unless you had a game. By the time we were ready for dinner, homework was done, and we can check it and they could read for another half hour before going to bed."

How engaged were you in your children's school?

Parent A: "I visited their schools. From elementary school, kindergarten to grade one, I took them to school. They need you with them; it builds their confidence to stay in school. I chaperoned school activities and did read-aloud for the elementary school ones. I attended most school activities though it is now tougher with my studies, but I make sure that I do all that I can do."

Parent B: "When the kids were younger, we used to go to awards ceremonies, report conferences, open house, and PTA meetings, bake sales, and did the fundraiser. After a while, we decided to just give the money for the candies because it was too much [interviewee's children attended a parochial school that had a lot of fundraisers to help support the school]."

Interviewer to Parent B: Why did your children attend Catholic schools?

Parent B: "We had no idea of public school when our children started school. Our oldest child started out at [parochial] school, which was close to where we lived as students. Besides, it was due to the idea that most of us went to Catholic school at home."

Parent C: "I coordinated parents' activities, helped other parents' [children] by tutoring them in Math, I taught African dance and I showed African culture and catered African food for school activities. I also chaperoned school activities. That helped my children, myself, and other children despite my busy life working and going to school. My kids like that also because it shows them that I cared about them and their education."

Parent D: "In the pre-school years, for the older kids when I was in school, being a fulltime mother and student, we visited every teacher they had. My husband and I purposely gave our children long Igbo names. I would visit the classroom and the teacher will gather all the children on the floor and tell them that Mrs. … is going to teach them how to say my children's names. I would teach the kids and teachers how to say my children's names and the meaning of the names. I will tell the children that everybody cannot be 'Jessica' or 'Paul' and inform them that there is a bigger world out there and not to make fun of my kid's names. My kids felt happy and were not ashamed of their names. When I had the opportunity, the [older] children were in Catholic schools. We paid for everything. These schools have their own ways. You paid for your kids to participate in programs. The other [younger] children, we experimented with the public school. When they had the Black History Month program, I participated but being a teacher myself it was difficult to schedule and hard for me. I had to schedule it early in the morning so that I could go to work after. I went in and trained the teachers and gave them a tape of the activities. My child was proud, and I saw my child feeling so proud. It helps to boost the ego and morale of the children. It helps teachers and everybody to respect the children. It was done in the auditorium and everybody participated. They saw our culture. The advantage as far as the young kid is concerned was that you feel respected and important and it helps to motivate [them]. It was a positive thing. It was a one-time thing, and it is not possible for the entire parent to do that. But for special things, I encourage parents to participate."

Parent E: "With the school, my first involvement was the parents-teachers conferences in the elementary school. I attended several parent report card conferences, picked up report cards and talked to teachers. Every school they attended, I visited and did a program about Africa and attended birthday parties of my children. I was involved in elementary and high school. I did programs for Black History month on storytelling and music. I participated in the fundraiser. In the … Club, I walked to help raise funds for my daughter's team."

Parent F: "With all of them we made it a duty to be engaged. With the first and second ones, we lived in a city and we had the opportunity to go for report card conferences whether the kids were doing good or bad. We wanted to know their teachers and ask questions. Being that they were in football and matching band in high school, I was involved in the band parents selling things at the concession stand at band events, did bake sales, and traveled with the group at competitions. With the third child, we moved to this suburb. We always struggled with the fact that they [the suburban school] did not have parent conferences during report card in this school district..."

Do you belong to Nigerian associations, and if so, why?

Parent A: "Yes, I belong to the Yoruba community. It is our culture, to help our children understand where they came from and to encourage with their education by providing free SAT lectures. The group facilitates free SAT prep for their children and the larger community."

Interviewer to Parent A: Who does the SAT lectures and is it open to anyone?

Parent A: "We have volunteers from the high schools and some Yoruba kids are also part of it. We want them to be familiar with their teachers [Nigerian volunteers]. The class is open to anyone in the community as well as our kids."

Parent B: "Yes, I belong to two groups [women's group and Nigerian village of origin ethnic group], primarily for social support."

Parent C: "Yes. These organizations help me to contribute my input on how to help the people back home. They send medications that people at home need."

Parent D: "We led the movement to initiate the formation of associations when we first arrived in the U.S. because we have only one life to live. I believe that at every stage of your life you should make the most of it. When I started college here, I started looking for the Nigerian Catholic community. The opportunity came to worship in Igbo in our parish and I was excited, and I started calling all the Nigerians. People were reluctant and said that I have brought this church thing to here. Even though I was going to school, I told them not to worry about interpreting the Bible in Igbo. My motivation was that wherever you are you do your best. I was doing the same things in Nigeria, participating in things in the community. I took that idea knowing that human life begins with baptism and you are supposed to be involved. That is why it did not discourage me. There are other [Nigerian groups] but they are not as enriching as the church. Sometimes I must handle things because if you leave it to people it will not work. The church is where I started. Then I had the Igbo program where I had the chance to reach others like the children and to national and international audiences. So, I did not have the time to join others because I like facilitating things. After a couple of years, the town things (town associations or groups) started forming but I did not like to join all these groups because we had children and I preferred the church group for my children. Later, I joined the local government group. I did join but I like creating things that can be duplicated. I have helped other associations to replicate things and sometimes people think I am a member of a group because I spend my money to help other groups. I help other associations to replicate what I do because it helps to further the culture. My program motivates other groups because we all want our traditions to continue."

Parent E: "Yes. I used to belong to several others, but I am not active in them anymore. I joined the associations for the social network, which I enjoy. It is an avenue to do something for people back home [in Nigeria]. I believe in causes and in helping people less fortunate. I enjoy being with people from the same place. It helps to keep me feeling good."

Parent F: "Yes, I belong to one. I joined the organization just for social interaction with our people. I joined for myself and knowing we are in a society where we struggle with our kids about who they will marry. We hope that our children will meet people from their backgrounds also."

Do you expose your children to Nigerian people and culture?

Parent A: "Yes, for the reasons cited previously."

Parent B: "We try to expose the children whether they learn anything from it is a different story. I do that because I believe that I am a Nigerian and so are they."

Parent C: "Of course, I do because it will help them in the future to realize that they don't belong only in America and that they have other cultures they can learn from. In school when they ask them about other cultures that they know, they will be able to say what they know about Nigeria. It will also expose them to other communities [other Nigerian communities]."

Parent D: "Yes, for the reasons cited previously."

Parent E: "Yes, definitely, I do take them to Nigerian events, cultural celebrations, and parties. I expose them to Nigerian culture in the house and to Nigerian people. When I call home [Nigeria], they talk to the people at home. All these things connect them to the culture."

Parent F: "Yes, very much so. We expose them to our culture mostly at home by speaking the language to them, teaching them certain things we were brought up with. It is a struggle for them because they are caught in two cultures and they often wonder why they have to do things the Nigerian way rather than the American way."

Have you ever experienced any problem with your children's school?

Parent A: "Never! It depends on you and the kids. If you let your kids understand the purpose of school, and that it is to learn, not to make friends or disturb the class, they will not have any problem with their teachers. They must respect teachers not just their parents. They need to understand the importance of being where they are. No teacher will pick on them if they were well behaved."

Interviewer to Parent A: What do you mean by the importance of being where they are?

Parent A: "That they are going to school to acquire an education and knowledge, not to play, distract others or for fun. They have no reason to disturb if they understand the purpose of being there [i.e., in school]. I always remind my children that I do not want the teacher to call me because they were rude or not behaving in school. Because of that, they are conscious of what they do because they know that I do not want to be called. I believe that if children are disciplined, they will be well behaved."

Parent B: "Not really."

Parent C: "None, probably because of their good behaviors and the teachers came to like them. Maybe because I am an active parent, and the teachers knew me, and my kids knew that I am involved and didn't get in trouble and have me come into the school."

Parent D: "None! My children have never experienced problems with other kids or the teachers in their school. They are so proud and often lecture other kids in the class about the world because they know a lot. Other kids look ignorant in class. They come out being proud and talk about the world and where they have been to. Teachers are also impressed about their knowledge of the world. Many of the kids they went to school with have not been on an airplane and have not traveled. We used to visit home [Nigeria] every four years and they would talk about stopping over in Italy and other countries, so other kids did not have a chance to look down on my kids. In high school, my oldest son had gone to a small town with his volleyball team to play and students from the small town, which was mostly white, looked down on his school, which was urban, and mostly minority population. It was not personal to him, but my son took it upon himself to do something about it. My son and the principal complained to the other school."

Parent E: "No. I never had any academic difficulties that pitted me against the school administrations."

Parent F: "No, I have never experienced any such thing where the kids are going to school. Also, partly I may say that because of the way our children were brought up. They know that misbehaving in school is unacceptable. I will take it back. My oldest one, when she started first grade was one of a few Blacks in her class. Her teacher told us that she was daydreaming a lot in class and we felt that she was trying to label her. We went into the school and told her that if our child was daydreaming, she was bored with whatever she was teaching her. We made her realize that she should not play with us. Even though my son was a troublemaker, I was never called into the school by the principal or the assistant principal. I never had that experience."

Who are your children's school friends?

Parent A: "Yes, I know the friends of my children and I know that they came from good homes because I try to know their parents and where they come from."

Parent B: "I know their friends and I met them at school and a few of them they brought home."

Parent C: "They have a combination of friends, African-Americans, Latinos, everybody. My kids are not racists. They pick their friends from different groups but not the crazy kids. They select their friends and communicate with everybody but the way I raised them; they do not like to hang out with people. They like to come home to their mother and stay away from trouble. For their birthdays, they invite their friends and they all come here."

Parent D: "Here, they have so many friends. In [previous state they resided] before we came [here], the children of our fellow Igbo Nigerians were their friends as we went to family events [together]. More than 80% of their friends are classmates where they go to school. After we moved here, my oldest daughter lost her early childhood friend. Their friends are often from the school. One of my daughters has a friend who is Caribbean. Most of their friends are school friends and are from immigrant families. From the Catholic Igbo Community, they see the kids there as relatives. For Nigerian activities, they expect you to organize everything but with the school friends they will initiate it."

Parent E: "Their friends are mostly minorities, like themselves. They are mixed also with some diversity. Some of their friends are Asians, Whites, and Latinos. This is more so for the younger ones who were born here. The older ones who were born in Nigeria tended to have friends who are Blacks whereas the last two have mixed friends."

Interviewer to Parent E: Why do you think that they chose their friends differently?

Parent E: "The two younger ones went to a multicultural school in an urban school district that reflected the diversity of the city. The older ones went to school in a white school. They had just recently come from Nigeria and were teased a lot and it affected them in making friends [choice of friends]. So, they were affected and most of their friends tend to be second-generation immigrants like them and they tended to relate more to them. The younger ones were born here and didn't need to adapt."

Parent F: "Each of them had a different set of friends. With the girls, most of their friends have an immigrant background. With my son, most are Americans, not children from an immigrant background." "I can't say why. Often, they pick their friends. It was more of academics for them rather than children of immigrants or not."

How do you motivate your children to do well in school?

Parent A: "I stay close to them, show them love, passion. When they get their report cards, they are so excited and would say 'mom, I got straight "A" what would you give me?' I buy them things to reward them for working hard not to bribe them. When they get a B+ on a test or as a grade in a marking period, they would tell me and seek my opinion about whether it will affect them at the end of the year and about how they can go about bringing the grade up because they know that I expect good grades and that I will reward them."

Interviewer to Parent A: Do you tell your children the stories your mom told you about the value of education growing up or do you change them?

Parent A: "I always tell them the truth about the stories my mom told me. My mom always took me to the hospital and showed me doctors and would tell me 'when you read your book, you wear hilly shoes [high heels], walk smart and get a good husband and home but if you do the other way you get nothing'. She often said, 'work when you are supposed to work and play when you are supposed to play' [there is time for everything]."

Parent B: "Whenever the kids receive an award such as honors, student of the month, we took them out to dinner."

Parent C: "We take them out for lunch, to the movies, give them money, and buy them things they need when they do well in school. I talk to them and tell them that life was not easy for us growing up in Nigeria..."

Parent D: "When we were in …, I had a chart of who did what. It was more of combining chores with schoolwork and things they should do. They had chores to be done. Some motivations we used included money, Broadway Shows but I set the expectations so high that there were few Broadway trips..."

Parent E: "One of the things I do happily is lie a lot, which is what I do to the class that I teach. I tell them that things are mandatory to get a good grade and are important. So, telling the white lies is what I did. Sometimes doing it with them so that it will look like a play instead of work."

Parent F: "We usually give them money, financial rewards, or take them to dinner or shopping. Let us say they wanted a game like Nintendo, and we would say ok you did well in school so let us go and get the game you wanted. Most of the time, it was a financial reward and of course a big hug."

How is education in Nigeria different from education in the United States?

Parent A: "In Nigeria, education is more difficult because here, there is more technology. When I was in Nigeria, I did not get to use the computer until I was in the university. Again, in terms of people who study medicine, they do more hands-on learning here than in Nigeria."

Parent B: "If things are running well in Nigeria, Nigerian education is stricter, more focused even though they don't have all the amenities they have in the U.S."

Parent C: "They have more opportunities here than in Nigeria, more access, and more resources that the government provides to students [in K-12 education]. Education in the U.S. is better because they break everything down and you can focus on one, like Science or Math. Unless you reached advanced education in Nigeria that's when you start choosing your career."

Parent D: "Comparing education in Nigeria and in the U.S. is like comparing apples and oranges. With Nigerian education, we lack resources, endure more hardship, and the... Parents approach education in Nigeria seriously because parents know that education leads to better life. Parents know and expect that their children will do more than the parents. Igboland is different. I do not like Nigerian society to be compared with the U.S. There are people here in the U.S. who approach education differently. In Nigeria, we tried to be like the white man by learning their culture. Some people in America approach education with hatred because of what the white man has done to them [Black youths' oppositional identity]. The way Nigerians approach education, the teacher is a god and kids go to school to learn but Nigerian children did not have ... [lack of resources]. It is unfair to compare it because so many opportunities are not there in Nigeria. Any of the negatives in Nigeria is due to lack of opportunities and the corruption in Nigeria is also messing up the education because teachers who are not paid leave their jobs to find something to do to feed their families. Because we did not have the opportunity, the people celebrated you when you went further with your education. Even to go from the village to the city was celebrated because it meant progress. They are in constant search for more opportunities. People will give their kids to relatives living in the city so that their children would have an opportunity to go to school. Parents in Nigeria believe that education takes place in the school. Readiness at home was to get your kids ready with supplies and feed them before they go to school. There was only one way to go and that was to pass your WASC [high school exit exam in Nigeria]. If you did not pass JAMB [college entrance exam in Nigeria], there was no opportunity and no future for you. So, people invest money and time to do well in their education in Nigeria. How many children [in the U.S.] go to Barnes and Noble to look for books to prepare for college? We have to pay to learn something and to gain knowledge, and confidence [in Nigeria]."

Parent E: "There are differences in what is taught. There is a poverty of resources in Nigeria in the form of teachers, buildings, and technology. Where we beat them is the question of students. Nigerian students are more focused and hungrier for knowledge and want it. They are eager to learn and work for it. Here you preach, cajole, and the students are laid back."

Parent F: "The education in the United States compared to Nigeria right now? Nigerian education now is a problem because of the number of days students spend in school. Most of the time, the universities are closed because of the strikes and you can see it from the communication from university students. When they communicate with you, when they write you, you can see that college kids in Nigeria have a problem constructing sentences not because of them but because of the government, school, and teachers. Teachers are not paid and so do not spend enough time in schools. Teachers have no supplies. The educational system in Nigeria is broken. They [teachers] are always on strike and in school for a few months and they would come back and give students exams on something they did not learn. There is no stability right now [in the Nigerian educational system]."

"If you were to experience any problems with your child's school, how would you handle it?"

Parent A: "I have not experienced any problems but if I were to experience it, I would try to understand how the problem came about. Maybe the teacher naturally picks on my child because of the color. After I have identified the problem, then I will know how to handle it."

Parent B: It depends on what the problem is. If it is about God knows unfair treatment, I would approach the teacher and take it to the school authorities if it is about not treating my child fairly.

Parent C: "Like I said earlier, I never had a problem with the schools. But if I did, I would have a consultation, set up a meeting with the teacher and the principal, and explain what my child told me and that I want to know what contributed to it. I will try to get to the cause and effect and whether my child was not doing what he is supposed to do and why I wasn't told earlier and why the teacher used a certain language if that was the case. I will start with the teacher first and then the principal."

Parent D: "Being an educator myself, I have always known that no teacher is out there to hurt my child but at the same time I don't take things for granted. Depending on what it is, I will gather as much information as possible, listen to my child's side of the story and distinguish how objective and subjective the child is, listen to the teacher, and from what the teacher is saying, it will help me to understand. Knowing my children, I know that they will not disrespect a teacher. They know that and will not come home if they did. The sensitive part is showing racist behavior, but I will turn it into a learning opportunity. I will go to the school and make sure that the teacher or students will understand. Knowing what I know I will use it as a teaching moment. I will prepare well, not humiliate anybody but use knowledge to clear the misconceptions. The goal is not for my child to feel good, but I will use it to make sure that they learn as well and I will start with the classroom but if it reaches the entire school, that's good too."

Parent E: "It depends on the problem. If the problem is related to a teacher, I have no difficulty going to the teacher. I try not to be emotional because I believe that whatever I heard I will need to verify it. I had to verify what the child is telling me because sometimes it could be self-serving on the part of the child. I would have to verify it and if it is true, I can take it to the principal to resolve the matter."

Parent F: "By going straight to the teacher as demonstrated earlier."

Do you think that Nigerians are generally academically successful?

Parent A: "Yes because Nigerians are determined and have integrity like principles. If you want to do something, you must do that thing. We use our own initiatives because we are determined. If we really want to do something or achieve a goal, we don't relent until we achieve it."

Parent B: "I think so if they focus on education. Also, Nigerians are academically successful because most Nigerians here came to study on a scholarship. And the scholarship then was not given because we love you but because they were academically equipped [that is merit-based]. Those who came on these scholarships did well when they got here." This also supports research on high selectivity of Nigerian immigrants in America which affects the outcomes of their children as seen in this research and previous researchers such as Massey et al. 2007.

Parent C: "I don't know about all Nigerians, but some of them. Maybe, those who want to be academically successful have made it. People have individual problems, so I do not want to categorize. I do not want to judge people. I know some people who have the opportunity have made it. It is an individual thing."

Parent D: "I would say that at least 60% of Nigerians are academically successful. Nigerians are successful because if you look at the Igbos who have been displaced in Nigeria, the best have left and are here. The Igbos that left were in search of an education. We have come here because we could afford to go to school, and I know a lot of Nigerians that came in the 1980's who can't go back. Yes, because Nigerians are determined and have integrity like principles. What else can two people with college education do other than give their children a good education? I tell my kids that they are coming from a home where the two parents have above college education and that they must perform. The Igbos are successful because they came here to further their education. Those that are coming now are even professors. They are not going to go lower. Some are doctors and nurses, and they have their goals and dreams, and these are the people on top of the society before they came here. There are others who come today to make money and to trade and without a college education and are mostly from the non-Igbo groups because the Igbo people in Nigeria do not easily get these kinds of visas."

Parent E: "Yes, I believe so strongly that Nigerians are generally academically successful because I see it. I see them and they tend to pop up everywhere I look so I believe they are successful people. They are aggressive in pursuing their goals."

Parent F: "Yes, in general, Nigerians are academically successful. We can see it from how well some of us are placed in society, even in the American society. If you go to any city or town, you see it. There are so many Nigerians that are highly placed in cities, towns, and big corporations. I will say that Nigerians are doing well academically." It is not surprising that youth and parents share similar views about Nigerians as academic high-achievers.

How much control do you have over the academic successes and failures of your children?

Parent A: "I have some control and I would take some credit but not all because it is easy to take the horse to the river, but you can't force it to drink. I may do all I said I do but if the children do not have the interest, they will not succeed in school. So, I congratulate them for listening to me and for doing well in school. My role is just to support them and to elevate them. It is up to them to lift themselves up."

Interviewer to Parent A: Tell me about your son. "Did you say that he decided to go to another high school?"

Parent A: "Yes, he said that he found out that … [the current school] had a health magnet for students interested in medicine and nursing and since he wants to be a doctor, the new school will be more practical than … (his other high school). So, he decided to change' and I supported him after finding out about the school, I realized that all he said about the school was true, so I supported him."

Interviewer to Parent A: How did he find out about the school?

Parent A: "Through his friends attending. My nephew and niece attended the school and graduated from the school. My nephew is a pharmacist, and they told my son about the school."

Interviewer to Parent A: If somebody asked you why Nigerian kids are doing well in school; how would you respond to that?

Parent A: "I would say that it is our culture. Our culture matters a lot and that is why I love our culture. Like I said earlier, Nigerians are determined people. Most Nigerians love education and have pride not in putting their shoulder up but in what they are and in what they do. So, for education, we are always willing to work hard. Being a full-fleshed Nigerian, we are always encouraging our children in education because it is a step to success."

Parent B: "I don't think I have all the control. The children contributed to it. I will not take all the credit because you can't force it when they don't listen."

Interviewer to Parent B: How do you find out what motivates the kids?

Parent B: "At times, the kids will do what you ask them to do because you are the parents, depending on their friends."

Interviewer to Parent B: Are you implying that parents monitor their children's friends as a way of getting them to achieve in school?

Parent B: "Yes, it is very important."

Interviewer to Parent B: How do you monitor their friends?

Parent B: "I always ask them if their friends did their homework today and I monitored the phone calls they get to know who was calling and why the person was calling. Is the person having the same problem with the homework as my child and the homework was being discussed? Also, going to the mall was forbidden in my house unless

179

you were going to buy something. You do not go to the mall to start walking around as some people do in this country. You go to the mall to shop."

Parent C: They do most of it themselves. All I do is just watch and guide them. They input more into their own education. Practically, they are on their own. They work individually and sometimes, they help each other. I just give advice and I watch if things are slowing down, I help push it up. Like right now that they just came back from school and they are resting. If by 6:00 pm homework did not start, I will ask. They are matured kids, and they think I don't watch but they know what to do."

Interviewer to Parent C: What advice would you give to other parents whose children are not doing well?

Parent C: "You have to sit the kids down and find out the problem. If the problem is with the kids, work with them and if it is with the teacher, go to the teacher. Also, encourage the kids and tell them that education is important. Reduce the extra-activities like sports. Americans support sports for Black people, but you cannot succeed in college without knowledge. Academics are more important than sports."

Parent D: "We are lucky that we have children who listen to us. If there is any credit, we knew that the beginning of any youth is the fear of God. That is why we wanted to raise our children the way we were raised in Nigeria, with the fear of God. They listened and were not influenced by others. The only credit is that we set our goals. Living in …[City], there was no outside help, so we had to set our goals. Before we even had children, we decided that I should take a job that would allow me to be there for the kids. My husband sacrificed his career to be there for the children. It was not easy, but we sacrificed for them. We set the goals too high so that they would not fall too far [down]. There was never a time that we were not available to them. We also put in money in them [paid for parochial education]. The school they were going to [attend] was important to us. It must be that they were hearing the same message from home at school. We had a routine and ate dinner together and they knew that dinner was fufu and everybody ate the same thing. We had communication and celebrated birthdays, special occasions together. We would sit at the dinner table and everybody sees each other's faces. We always ate dinner together. It was the thing to do because for breakfast everybody grabs what they could, and they eat lunch at school. The school they went to have a lot to do with shaping their characters."

Interviewer to Parent D: Do you or did you have any child in public school?

Parent D: "I have two in … (public magnet school). Two are doing elementary school there. The difficulties in our lives have made it difficult for them." [husband suffered a serious health setback]. It is not fair to them and they should be exposed to what the (other siblings) had experienced. The youngest one never went to a Catholic school, but the influence of the older ones rubs off on her. My oldest daughter has taken over and they all listen to her. She does not talk much, but she is like a god in her quiet ways. My youngest one looks up to the older ones and adores them. The influence that the older ones got from the Catholic school is showing in the younger ones."

Parent E: "I have never thought of it that way in terms of percentage. I will consider my part very insignificant may be 20%. My children are self-driven because they are not the type to ask, 'Did you do your homework'? Even if I was not there, they will do their homework so I will give myself no more than 20% over their academic success."

Parent F: "I think just giving them the basics when they were little and teaching them the right way of doing things and letting them know what they had to do. I cannot say we have total control over their successes because we live in a society where kids have freedom and control. It was by the grace of God. When they are not in the house, we can't control what they do but maybe the basics we gave them helped them to be where they are today."

In summary, some of the parents were navigating their own education in American colleges and job terrains while simultaneously navigating through the K-12 educational terrains for their children. They were having and raising children concurrently as they improved their education. They also dealt with underemployment and racial discrimination at work, but never lost sight of their children's education and made sacrifices to send them to parochial schools for better educational outcomes and religious instruction. While youth participants credited their parents for their academic success, parents interviewed passed most of the credit to their children. Unmistakably, parents revered and viewed education as the pathway to success and preached what I named the *gospel of education creed* to their children. It is obvious that the parents' responses reflect where their children's drives, self-efficacy, and optimism came from.

CHAPTER 11

Message to Nigerian Parents from Second-Generation Nigerians in the Study

I will be remiss if I fail to communicate the concerns of the second-generation youth regarding their Nigerian parents, as some of what the younger generation shared could provide a guideline for Nigerian parents raising kids in the U.S. today. Some of the participants made it clear that I should communicate their thoughts to Nigerian parents through their excitement for this study and their suggestions about how to improve the study and ideas for future research. Youth in the study extolled their parents for raising them with a Nigerian identity and for instilling the Nigerian culture, value for education, strong work ethic, and self-efficacy in them. They agreed that the keyword to describe their upbringing is *strict*. Although they did not like the strictness of their parents as young people, as they got older, they came to accept the value of having such an upbringing and credited their academic achievements to their parents. They eventually valued the motivation, support, routines, structure, sacrifices, and the way they were brought up as evident throughout this book.

However, the main concern most participants shared was the problem of Nigerian parents pushing their children into certain fields without regard to the child's interest or passion. The problem may stem from the fact that high-achieving second-generation Nigerian youth excel in all academic fields, as many high-achieving students often do. As a result, their parents assume that if they excel in the biological sciences, for example, they should be physicians or nurses. This can create mental anguish for the children when they start exploring other interests in college and find out that they really have no desire for whatever their parents have planned for them. Two youth shared with me their internal conflicts and struggles as they attempted to share with their parents that they would change their major from pre-med to something else. For one of them, the price was the loss of time toward graduation and some "mental anguish," though the parents were ultimately supportive of the change given the alternative. One of the focus-group participants has this to say about her experience regarding Nigerian parents: "Some Nigerian parents are bad. I know of a whole family that does not get along. The parents are strict but went overboard in being extreme. The siblings hate each other and compete against each other. I know of one student who would not go home because the father would not approve of the student's major." This type of toxic family dynamics could have been created by parents pitting siblings against each other by comparisons and intense competition. As mentioned earlier, one participant talked about a second-generation Nigerian youth who committed suicide due to academic pressure from his parents. No achievements would be worth destroying a family bond or losing a child. As an educator for over thirty years, I witnessed what such pressures did to some young second-generation youth from various racial backgrounds.

Therefore, the first message from second-generation Nigerian youth is that while they value the parental high expectations and push to do well in school, they would like explicit support in following their passions towards their true calling. That also means that if the youth chooses not to attend an elite college, that is not the end of the world. As I often told the parents of my high school students as a teacher and administrator, it is not the school or degree but what you do with it. Many successful African-Americans are graduates of the Historically Black Colleges and Universities and opt to send their children to these schools because graduates of those schools graduate with an education that prepares them for leadership and successful careers in American society without assaulting their racial identity. All successful people did not attend an elite college, and all elite college graduates are not successful. Many Nigerian immigrants are successful, but we did not attend Ivy League colleges. Many second-generation Nigerians would likely end up in career fields that are not even available today, so parents should allow their children to explore their passions and dreams. When people follow their passion, success, and status are more likely to follow. As parents, the only thing you owe the children is to educate and help them explore the many possibilities available to them. Many second-generation Nigerian youth in America are now making names for themselves in professional sports, television, entertainment, literary, and other fields by following their passions. After all, America is the land of opportunity where dreams can come true.

The second message involves the Nigerian associations and conventions where families gather to socialize with each other and raise funds for those in need, both in Nigeria and in their communities in the United States. Participants spoke favorably about such gatherings and Nigerian communities, including religious ones. They enjoyed the cultural socialization but wished that such gatherings included more youth-friendly activities at their events. They also wished that the parents taught them how to speak their native languages such as Igbo and Yoruba, to help them interact more with their Nigerian community and relatives. A suggestion is adding youth programs at Nigerian gatherings to reflect activities beyond dance and fashion shows, including language classes and having older second-generation youth discuss experiences from the college application process, their college education, their careers, and other topics that might be of interest to second-generation youth (like code-switching, which came up repeatedly in this study).

The third message is about identity issues. While some of the parents in the study were more open-minded about the identity affiliation of their children, some youth indicated that their parents did not want an ethnic or cultural affiliation with African-Americans (meaning Blacks without recent immigrant background or of Nigerian descent). Nigerian parents should understand the contextual nature of identities of their children who are Black and of immigrant background in a race-conscious America. Unlike many of their parents, second-generation Nigerians are aware of the African-American experience in America by attending K-12 schooling in the United States, sharing some cultural ties and closer proximity with African-Americans than their parents. As a result, they are likely to adopt a more pan-ethnic Black identity than their parents because they understand the multidimensionality of race as a concept. My interactions with many Nigerian parents living in America show that they have limited interactions with middle-and-upper-class African-Americans and some harbor the negative stereotypes of African-Americans portrayed on American media—just as some African-Americans harbor some negative stereotypes about Africans. Researchers have also found that immigrants seem to pick up the negative media stereotypes of African-Americans (Adeleke, 2004; Arthur, 2000; Traore, 2003).

Nevertheless, I observed that even as Nigerian-American youth endure some teasing from some African-American peers, many second-generation Nigerians believe that they have some affinity with African-Americans and take on that identity depending on the context. Second-generation Nigerians also use code-switching as a means of socializing with different groups, including African-Americans, something that many of their parents oppose. Second-generation Nigerian youth understood that this skill is used by many successful people. As mentioned, one youth reminded her parents that she spoke Ebonics to her African-American friends for the same reason Nigerians spoke Igbo, Yoruba, Pidgin, and English as needed. The reality is that without the accent as a marker and without disclosing their names, second-generation Nigerian youth are viewed as African-Americans in the United States and many of the youth understood that when they talked about the fluidity and contextual nature of identities.

The fourth message for Nigerian parents is to accept that second-generation Nigerians ultimately would define and even redefine success according to their experiences in America and on their terms, different from their parents. They may or may not be driven by status, pedigrees, or even money. They are growing up in a country that is boundless in terms of the opportunities available to them in comparison to their immigrant parents. They also are socially aware due to the injustices surrounding race and poverty in U. S society, and they may seek fulfillment through public service and non-profit sectors. Many of the youth in the study expressed interest in community service and making a difference in the public sector. They have been exposed to the long history of injustice in America by attending American schools their entire lives and they may have personally experienced racial injustice or know people who did. This makes them particularly aware that their careers could influence change in America. Success to second-generation Nigerians could mean finding happiness in making the world, including the United States, a better place. As shown in this study, their goals are not fixed but always shifting as they learn more about themselves and the world. Creating the next app or next social media platform might be their primary aspiration. It is not inconceivable that the next Jeff Bezos, Bill Gates, or Mike Zuckerberg could be second-generation Nigerians in the United States, where the horizon belongs to them.

The final message and perhaps the most important one is the issue of bullying in the schools. Some of the participants in the study shared that they were bullied by both white and Black students, sometimes, more so by Black students. They were particularly upset about being bullied by African-Americans whom they expected to be their allies. One youth said she was so upset about being bullied that she wanted to fight but knew her parents would not tolerate it. Even as they bring home excellent grades, the children may suffer long-lasting emotional scars from being victimized by bullies. Nigerian parents need to be vigilant about the emotional wellbeing of their children to detect and help the children deal with this challenge. Earning good grades could mask the problem, so parents should ask their children about more than grades when the children get home from school. Questions about whether anyone has bothered them in school can help open the door to hear about the child's experiences. Some children might not open up without a prompt from their parents. As a school administrator, I took the issue of bullying seriously, knowing that some children commit suicide because of it. It has become more pervasive with the myriad social media available to children today; most of the peer conflicts I dealt with as a school administrator stemmed from online bullying. I have seen firsthand how cruel teenage girls and boys can be to their peers on social media. One thing Nigerian parents must not do is to discount the experience when the children do share about being bullied. As parents, our children look to us to protect them. No child should have to endure bullying, and as parents, we must intervene and do what is needed to stop it including, bringing it to the attention of the school and teaching our children how to protect themselves as many of the youth in the study did.

CHAPTER 12

Message to Educators in the United States

I write this message to educators at all levels but more so to PreK-12 educators. As a retired public-school educator with more than three decades of experience in an urban setting, I learned a lot about what makes students successful both as a teacher and as an administrator. My experiences as a Black mother of highly educated and successful children also inform what I have to say here. I genuinely believe that most teachers, whether in private, parochial, or in public schools, want to do well with their students but often do not know how to deal with minority children. I know this because I worked with many teachers in an urban school setting for more than thirty-two years as their peers and as an administrator. This message is not directed exclusively at white teachers, as some minority teachers can use this message as well. I have known effective and not-so-effective teachers of all races as I grew into the profession. I have also worked with excellent white teachers of minority students, and some of these teachers had been my mentors. Nothing you learn during your teacher in-service training can adequately prepare anyone to be a effective teacher, especially in an urban setting where some students arrive with insurmountable challenges—but at least they show up. They show up because they want to learn and experience success despite their challenges. As a teacher, you can make or break a child's future trajectory. That is a lot of power in your hands. Please use it judiciously. As a school administrator, I witnessed a teacher attempt to prevent a student from earning a high school diploma because they had a disagreement, and I fought it with all my might. Teachers must separate the action from the child and remember that children need love when they least deserve it, according to one popular saying. My motto was always to treat my students as I would want my children treated. Our real test as educators is how we educate the most challenging students, not those who can educate themselves with our minimal help. I also celebrate good teachers and strongly believe we should have Academy Awards-style recognition for teachers. After all, teaching serves as the grandparents to all other professions.

I particularly wanted to address teachers in this book because teachers hold the future of our society through their early influence on children. For children from all backgrounds with challenging home environments, teachers can make the difference between life and death, or between prison and progress (through of course interventions with social agencies in extreme situations when the lives of children are in danger at home). When all children succeed, America will be better for it. Educators must take the role of shaping the future of America seriously. Here is an unordered list of what I wish all teachers would keep in mind as they work with minority students from marginalized groups.

1. Keep in mind that all parents love their children and have dreams, hopes, and goals for their children and that includes parents of all ethnic groups.

2. All children start school with a natural curiosity and eagerness to learn but somehow many minority children lose it along the way. Teachers have a professional obligation to make sure they

do not contribute to extinguishing the burning desire to explore that children bring to school. They owe it to the children, parents, society, and to the profession. To better engage minority children, teachers should incorporate multi-cultural education in their curriculum. All it takes is the will and a Google search. Nothing ignites students' passion for learning more than learning about what interests them.

3.   Please do not judge children by their skin color, ethnicity, their names, or any other markers of otherness. Foreign, black-sounding names, or other differences do not signal less intelligence. I know of cases where a teacher told a Nigerian professor that his daughter could not earn an A in English because they are foreigners and I personally experienced that with one of my children. I know of Nigerian doctors and professors whose children began school reading well above their grade-level being told by teachers that their children were not ready for school, unmotivated, restless, etc., when in fact the children were bored to death in class. The parents, of course, fought back because they are educated and know their children. Just think about poor and Black children with less-educated parents in America and you can see how this could have ended up with children being stigmatized and labeled. This scenario helps explain why many Black children end up being labeled and placed in special education in American schools.

4.   Get to know your students and build positive relationships with them. Every child is different and unique with their strengths and weaknesses, as we all have. Guide them to build up their strengths in their class activities and assignments, giving them a chance to experience success, which often leads to more success.

5. Please do not be afraid of Black children or Black parents. Instead, keep an open line of communication with them. They know when you mean well and when you mean well, you are more likely to do right by them and their children. That is not to say that you will not meet a difficult parent, but keep in mind that how you handle it determines whether the child will succeed in your class or not. The focus should be on the best interest of the child. As a professional, do not hesitate to remind disgruntled parents about that. As a professional, I always kept my focus on the child when dealing with difficult parents. However, parents should respect teachers as they work together for the best interest of their children. Children succeed when schools work with parents as a team.

6. Establish a positive relationship with students and parents early in the school year; be consistent, fair, and respectful while holding students accountable and you should have nothing or little to worry about. Students need structure to learn and they appreciate it from both parents and teachers. Remember to be human and yes, you can smile before December, contrary to the popular teacher myth. That is part of what makes you human to the students.

7. Your students will remember you many years later by how you treated them, more than by what you taught them. I have experienced that many times over. I wish I knew this when I began my teaching career.

8. Value the cultural backgrounds of your students and create a culture of respect in your classroom that celebrates the cultural diversity of your students. Your classroom should be a haven for your students to thrive. It is important to teach children that their

cultural background has value and that no culture is inferior or superior to another.

9. Watch the language you use in your classroom. Words like "dumb" communicate to children that it is okay to use derogatory words in talking about others. Model what you preach. Sarcasm has no business in the classroom. It prevents students from taking academic risks in the classroom.

10. It is not your place to discourage a student's dream regardless of how far behind you think the student may be. Your affirmation could be the single factor that will alter a child's fate and future. I had students who told me that my affirmation was the single factor that altered their lives. As educators, we never really know the impact we have on students until many years down the road.

11. Recognize that students learn differently and use a variety of instructional strategies, which are a Google search away in today's world. If teachers make learning accessible to students, they are more likely to succeed in school.

12. Give students a second chance to improve their grades. We all deserve a second chance in life and you never know what your students went through the night before or the morning of the test. When you have a problem at home, you would want your boss to take that into consideration in your workplace.

13. Be sure to reward students for their effort, not necessarily for being smart, to give them a sense of agency. You want to teach them that effort and hard work, not just natural talent, lead to success. It also teaches them to double their efforts when they fail, instead of giving up because they are not smart enough to alter the outcome.

14. Lay down the class rules with your students' input and hold them accountable to the rules with consistency and fairness. Although students like structure and fair-minded rules, they hate being singled out and often teachers want to make an example out of one person because of frustration. Avoid this at all costs.

15. Make detentions an opportunity to get to know the students better and an opportunity to make up missing work or other assignments as you deem fit. I always loved getting students to write a reflection about what they did wrong. It is an opportunity for students to think about the effects of their actions on others.

Finally, every educator has an obligation to help counter the plague of covert and overt racism endemic in American society. Children are not born racists but learn so from their homes and society. The soul of America's future will depend on how well our diverse multiracial society learns to respect each other and equally enjoy the great country they live in. Yes, there is still racism in America and many Black citizens have experienced it both knowingly and unknowingly. It exists at all levels of society. I recall that after I made the transition from an assistant principal to head of a magnet school, I was asked if I still thought there was racism in America. To this person, my promotion has erased any traces of racism in America, because as a Black immigrant with a doctorate (the only one in the school), I headed the district's flagship high school program. These kinds of attitudes transfer to children, who can then bring prejudice, stereotypes, and racism to school at a young age. My older daughter at age seven was told in class by her white classmate after she answered a question in class that her mother told her "Black people are dumb." To which my daughter responded, "Your mother must be dumb." The same daughter sat in an Ivy League university classroom and listened to a white student make a presentation using pseudo-science to explain how Blacks are genetically an inferior race, with the approval of the white professor. My child was numb with pain and anger; as a mother I was outraged. All my husband and I could do was console her with the knowledge she already had about the social construction of race. That experience made me understand and appreciate why many high-achieving African-American students might prefer Historically Black Colleges and Universities to the elite predominantly white colleges in the United States.

As educators, such scenarios in the classroom represent teaching moments to educate young people—unless the teacher honestly believes in the theory of superior versus inferior race that has been debunked over and over by science. Good teachers like parents seize every opportunity to teach. Teachers are like second parents to their students; when my students slip and call me "ma," I would tell them that while in my class, I was their mother and treated them accordingly. As an educator, I referred to my students as "my babies"—the same term of endearment I call my three children and grandbaby.

CHAPTER 13

Beyond the "Triple Package" Theory

I feel compelled to address the "Triple Package" theory because the authors of this theory (Chua & Rubenfeld, 2014) cited my work to make the case for their book about why some minority groups achieve at a high level in America. Groups named in their book included the following: Chinese, Jewish, Indian, Lebanese, Iranians, Cubans, Nigerians, and Mormons. The pair attributed the success of the groups to "superiority complex", "inferiority complex" and "impulse control." While such traits could apply to any individual of high achievement, they are insufficient explanations for the success of the groups, especially Nigerians. The authors did not take a deeper look at the complexities of Nigerian immigrants as they navigate their multiple experiences while striving to improve themselves in the United States as Blacks with high educational attainments. None of the groups identified in the Triple Package face the type of racism that Nigerians experience in America due to their skin color. All share some privileges of a social hierarchy due to their lighter skin colors and some share little in common with Nigerians beyond being immigrants. As Black Africans, Nigerian immigrants in the United States live with the inherent racial bias that classifies Blacks as biologically and intellectually inferior (Herrnstein & Murray, 1994) in the minds of some people. No other group listed has such an arduous challenge. In addition to the privilege of lighter skin color, some of the groups such as Cubans received a more welcoming support from the United States upon their arrival which laid the foundation for their future success (Portes & MacLeod, 1996; Portes & Rumbaut, 2001).

The Triple Package theory is an oversimplification of why these groups have been successful in America. There are multiple factors that account for why some groups succeed more than others in the United States, such as the selectivity and capital available to the group. Also, there are many people within the identified groups that do not become successful in America. Consequently, there is always the danger of perpetuating the myth of the model minority among certain ethnic groups with successful members (Kao, 1995; Suzuki, R. H., 1980). As a Nigerian parent, sociologist, and former educator in an urban public school for over three decades, I wanted to provide some of the contexts that were inadvertently omitted about Nigerian immigrants and their children as they seek to cross racial barriers while navigating American society. As stated earlier, Nigerians in the United States, irrespective of their high educational attainment level, are unlike any other groups profiled in "Triple Package." No other groups share the amount and level of prejudice and racial discrimination due to their skin color as Nigerians.

The idea of superiority complex would not apply to Nigerians in the United States as Nigerian immigrants do not share a common historical myth, religious or otherwise, that would engender any such feeling of superiority among them. They arrive in the United States with ethnic identities, and while they are a proud people with high achievement orientation, they lack the criteria that Chua and Rubenfeld described in their book, such as a religious or ancient mythical bond. Nigerians arrive in the United States not with a monotonous culture but rather with ethnic identity, and many Nigerian immigrants create social organizations in the United States based on such ethnic affiliations. For example, you might see an Igbo or Yoruba association in cities or metropolitan areas with a large Nigerian population. Many second-generation Nigerians would be unable to cite any historical reason to claim a feeling of superiority over any group of people that enabled them to succeed academically in America. Rather, what Nigerians possess is optimism, self-confidence with self-efficacy, and the attendant belief that they can accomplish, regardless of the challenges that come their way. Nigerians are resilient at home and abroad. Nigerians in America are not anxious about their status in America but rather hold a history of achievement orientation prior to immigrating to the United States. Consequently, the parents pass a history of generational achievement to their children. The need for achievement and high-status, coupled with their self-confidence and their high selectivity drive Nigerians to excel in the United States. They also lack ethnic enclaves and any structural support that some of the groups in the Triple Package Theory have in terms of being able to build businesses with ingroup financial support.

Therefore, I argue that the highly selective group of Nigerians in America, are primarily motivated to succeed by their optimism, rather than fear of failure. When I spoke to second-generation youth and their Nigerian mothers for my study, fear was not one of the key reasons why the youth strived for success. Anyone familiar with Nigerians knows that insecurity is not a word that can describe them. If anything, they are perceived to be grandiose, according to some of the youth in my study. Even with racism and discrimination in America, they are undeterred and seem to find a way out of their situation. When faced with underemployment and job discrimination, many start their own business. They do not sit around with their children discussing how oppressed or insecure Nigerians are to motivate their children to achieve, nor do they discuss the great Nigerian civilizations with their children to build their "superiority complex." Rather, Nigerian parents tell their children that they can do well in school and provide them with the necessary tools to do well. They tell their children that what anyone can do, they too can do it better.

As a Nigerian immigrant who has managed to achieve upper-middle-class status, my experiences, and those of many other successful Nigerian-Americans, show that such status does not shield us from racial discrimination; identifying us as a "model minority" masks the true experiences of Nigerian immigrants. Besides, it leads to more division amongst Blacks in the United States when we compare a few highly selected groups of people to a group with more than four hundred years of marginalization. Many of the groups mentioned as achievers could blend in with the dominant group if their religion is not mentioned. Some are associated with a "positive stereotype" if one may use the phrase (to me, no stereotype in positive), while Nigerians contend with many negative stereotypes about their ethnicity and race. This affects their ability to earn a professional living in the United States even with their high level of educational attainment.

Creating the illusion of "model minority" success for Nigerian immigrants with the groups listed negates the racial discrimination many Nigerians face in the United States and serves as a pacification for the discriminations they experience in the United States even with their outstanding educational attainment. Many Nigerian immigrants entering the labor force with high educational attainments nonetheless do not fare well in the job market. Research backs this up, showing that African immigrants are often underemployed and underpaid given their educational attainment levels (Butcher, 1994; Kposowa,

2002; Dodoo, 1997; Dodoo & Takyi, 2002; Model & Ladipo, 1996). Scholars and researchers should not continue to perpetuate the myth of model minorities, which can yield disastrous consequences for the minority groups identified as such. For example, Asians who fall short of the academic expectations that they are good at math lose their individuality (Tatum 1992) or worse. As an urban high school educator, I worked with students who were despondent over their poor academic performances and failure to meet up with the expectations assigned to their ethnic group.

During my interviews of second-generation Nigerian youth, they shared that they found that their experiences with parental strictness was comparable to other second-generation youth. That is the one thing I would say Nigerian youth might have in common with some of the immigrant groups in the triple package—though not with all the listed groups. Second-generation Nigerian youths' experiences with their mothers, for example, did not rise to the level of the "Tiger Moms" in the Asian culture, as Nigerian parents would not force their children to take violin or piano if the children were not interested. Rather, they encourage their children to engage in extra-curricular activities of their choice including sports as a means of getting into good colleges. For example, if playing soccer well would lead to being recruited by Harvard, then you should play your heart out, but you must bring home good grades. For Nigerian parents, once athletic participation interferes with good grades, then it is over no matter how much the kid loves the sports. Nigerian-style parenting is what my niece Ashley calls "Momma Bear." Nigerian mothers are highly protective of their children while maintaining high behavioral and academic expectations of them as they hover over them. But second-generation Nigerian youth have freedom with regards to which extra-curricular activities they partake in.

What we need is not more theories to justify the "model minority" paradigm that somehow indicts some minority groups who fail to achieve due to structural barriers they face in the United States. Rather, we need to start figuring out the multiple contexts that must come together to support all children in America to help them reach their full potentials. We need to create opportunities for all children and not just based on race, skin color, and the socio-economic status of their parents.

Like Nigerians, all the immigrant groups named in the triple package are a self-selected group and originated from countries that cannot claim to be "model countries." I propose that scholars examine how they use language to theorize about ideas that lead to the increased marginalization of some minority groups in the United States. In over three-decades as an urban educator, I have seen all the ramifications of the marginalization of groups as manifested in their children.

CHAPTER 14

Conclusion

Research on minority and marginalized youth seldom examines the contextualized nature of such populations as it affects their academic outcomes (Spencer et al., 1991). This book has examined the experiences of some high-achieving second-generation Nigerian youth to determine how they navigate their education and experiences through the multicontextual terrains of the United States. As mentioned earlier, Nigeria sends more immigrants to the United States than any other sub-Saharan African country, yet there is a dearth of research on how their second-generation children experience the educational landscape of the United States. To help all students succeed in their academic endeavors, we need to understand the experiences and backgrounds of high-achieving second-generation Nigerian youth. Also, this study tried to dispel the myth of Black academic inferiority frequently portrayed in the media (Slaughter-Defoe et al., 1990). Focusing solely on the challenges of a group without understanding how they negotiate their experiences to achieve success perpetuates the stereotype of defeatist and pessimist approach (Floyd, 1996), negating the human agency available to groups.

It appeared from my study that high-achieving second-generation Nigerian youth had developed resiliency in the way they responded to their challenges. They exhibited multicultural skills that allowed them to value their ethnic culture, with a mastery of the mainstream culture. They also possessed a repertoire of codes that they switched into when necessary. Access to social capital through their parents, schools, peers, and the Nigerian community helped to reinforce the value of education and academic achievement.

When students have access to people who support their goals, they have a better chance of succeeding in school. Schools need to work with parents to create opportunities for immigrant and minority students to succeed. When the multiple worlds of students of color are harnessed, tapping their multiple dimensional contexts, they are bound to succeed (Phelan et al., 1993). Educators and parents should empower such students with a sense of personal agency to embrace their ethnic culture and the mainstream culture or western cultural norms (Li, 2004) and the skills to navigate both worlds.

It was evident that the academic achievement of immigrant and minority youth could not be attributed to a single factor. High-achieving second-generation Nigerian youth in this study attributed their academic success to their internal motivation, their parents, and the social capital available to them through their community. Although Ogbu's cultural ecological theory (1987) was useful in understanding the academic experiences of these youth, students' agency and the ability to tap the resources in their social contexts also contributed to the academic success of the youth.

High-achieving second-generation Nigerian youth exhibited the characteristics of high-achieving students from other groups. They came from two college-educated parent homes where education was valued and emphasized. They also shared characteristics with other immigrant youth struggling to adapt to American culture while maintaining their ethnic identity and heritage. The fact that the youth in the sample held on to their Nigerian ethnicity could indicate that identity was an integral part of their academic success.

If so, the lesson here is that immigrant youth could retain their cultural heritage as social capital which can facilitate academic achievement, as evident in the findings of Matute-Bianchi (1986) and Gibson (1988). These researchers found that immigrant youth in their studies had learned to accommodate mainstream culture to the extent that such culture aided their adaptation; at the same time, the youth chose to preserve their ethnic cultures rather than subscribe to total assimilation to mainstream culture. High-achieving second-generation Nigerian youth believed that their upbringing and a Nigerian identity helped them to succeed in school. They had developed adeptness for negotiating across cultures through code-switching.

Unlike the high-achieving Black students in Fordham's (1988) study, who adopted a raceless identity as a strategy to achieve academic success, high-achieving second-generation Nigerian youth in this study embraced their ethnic and cultural identity. Rather than adopt a "raceless" identity, they adopted code-switching as a strategy for managing their academic experiences. Code-switching could have helped high-achieving second-generation Nigerian youth to deal with peer isolation and to lessen the burden of the 'acting white' phenomenon that often threatens the potential academic success of some Black youth.

This was particularly relevant because researchers (Ford et al., 1993; Fordham, 1988; Fordham & Ogbu, 1986) have found that managing academic achievement by Black students was often a difficult task, as these students often feel rejected by their peers. All youth do not manage their academic and peer challenges in similar ways. Research on different populations would assist researchers and educators in understanding what works for different groups. For high-achieving second-generation in this study, they intentionally selected their friends from peers with similar background and interests and removed themselves from peers deemed detrimental to their goals.

The findings of this study have implications for our schools and how we educate minority and immigrant youth. There is a need for our schools to embrace cultural pluralism and multicultural education if we are to adequately educate all youth for the 21st Century. This is especially important as the population of children of color aged 15-19 in our schools is projected to increase from 34% to 46% by 2025 (Kao & Thompson, 2003). Schools and our society need to appreciate the bicultural identities of immigrant youth and educate immigrant youth on how to negotiate such identities. Being different should never be deemed inferior, intellectually, or otherwise.

To be an American and to have a bicultural identity were not mutually exclusive for high-achieving second-generation Nigerian youth in this study. The youth held on to their ethnic identities while successfully pursuing the mainstream American aspirations through education. Preparing all youth for a multicultural society would also prepare youth for a multicultural globalized world. It is possible to educate all youth about how to negotiate multiple social contexts and educate teachers and society, in general, to be more accepting of multiculturalism in our schools and society. We must learn to coexist as members of a diverse nation.

Minority youth such as second-generation youth should be allowed to maintain a sense of multicultural identity without feeling that their culture is at odds with the mainstream culture (P. Portes, 1996b). Such youth could be taught code-switching strategies to cope with the multiple social environments they are expected to navigate in their lives. They could also be taught that being a minority and being academically successful are not mutually exclusive. As Li (2004) noted, second-generation youth should be helped to both maintain positive bicultural identity and mainstream cultural norms. The goal of educators should include teaching minority and immigrant students to acclimate to mainstream culture while preserving their ethnic identity. Being an American should not have to mean sacrificing one's ethnic and cultural identity. And neither should being an ethnic American nor being successful be mutually exclusive. Students can achieve academic success when schools and the community work in collaboration with families to support students (Phelan et al., 1998; Rhamie & Hallam, 2002).

Future research

High-achieving second-generation youth in the sample generously shared their experiences and offered several recommendations on possible areas to expand the scope of this study. Based on the sample for this study, second-generation Nigerian males were under-represented both in the individual and focus-group interviews, and more research is needed with male students in this group. Are second-generation Nigerian males experiencing unique challenges or is there under-representation because of sampling error? Some participants suggested that there might be a gender difference in the experiences of the second-generation Nigerian youth. Some Nigerian parents I know seem to believe from their experiences that the second-generation Nigerian girls perform better than their male counterparts in academic achievements, career aspirations, and eventual career attainments. Do second-generation Nigerian males face the same academic outcome as some African-American youth in the urban schools? If so, why? This needs further exploration.

Another area for future research is a comparison of the experiences of second-generation youth who attended racially diverse schools, and those who attended suburban non-diverse schools, to understand whether they are subjected to more teasing or bullying. It appeared that youth who attended urban parochial high schools did not endure much peer teasing but were generally underprepared for college. On the other hand, the youth that attended suburban schools were exposed to social isolation and racial teasing, even though they benefited from the academic rigor of the suburban school districts. Therefore, there was always a tradeoff regardless of the type of school the youth attended. A comparative study of second-generation Nigerian youth attending urban and suburban schools would shed more light on this finding.

The issue of parental pressure to pursue certain careers also demands further exploration. Is the idea of Nigerian parents steering their kids into trophy careers causing harm to the younger generation? Is there a maximum level, after which parental pressure and expectation become undesirable? These are some of the questions that future research can address. The story of a second-generation Nigerian youth who committed suicide over academic pressures needs to be further explored to determine if it is a common phenomenon among some of these youth. Does such pressure impact the mental health of the youth? This deserves further study.

Data analysis showed that all youth in this study attended a magnet urban high school, a parochial high school, or a suburban high school. A follow-up study could investigate how Nigerian parents decide on the type of K-12 schools that their children attend. When the issue of school choice came up, one parent, a schoolteacher and a devout Catholic started her children in a public school. When her first child attended public school as a first-grader after attending a Catholic preschool, her child came home crying about how badly behaved the children in her public school were. This parent had an epiphany and put all her children in Catholic school. Another parent indicated she knew little about public school when her oldest child started school. Her decision to send her children to a parochial school was based on the proximity of the school and her experiences attending a Catholic school growing up in Nigeria.

The sample for this study came from middle-class and upper-middle-class background. Consequently, it was difficult to determine whether the academic success of these youth was largely due to their socioeconomic background or due to the "Nigerian parents' factor," as the youth in the focus-group dubbed it. Further research would be needed to determine how much of the academic success of the youth were attributable to their socioeconomic background. However, a key observation was that these youth were highly motivated regardless of the socioeconomic status of their parents. Residence in an urban or suburban setting did not affect their level of motivation. All parents interviewed revered education and shared a belief in the gospel of education creed as the key to success—the same gospel they heard from their parents growing up.

One youth suggested that a follow-up study could explore how much of their academic success was attributable to their Nigerian cultural background. The youth in the study favored a Nigerian identity, whether as Nigerian-American or as Igbo or Yoruba. An important follow-up could examine the effects of Nigerian identity and the non-Nigerian identity on the academic outcomes of high-achieving second-generation Nigerians. Such a study could be extended to explore the identity of low-achieving second-generation Nigerian youth. It is possible that bicultural identity could serve as a protective factor for academic success for second-generation Nigerian youth in the United States. Many youth in the study alluded to the idea that Nigerian identity was instrumental to their academic success. This requires further investigation in future research.

Some youth indicated that they perceived differential parental expectations based on birth order and ability. It would be interesting to investigate whether Nigerian parents pushed their older children more than the younger ones or whether expectations were set for children based on innate ability and self-motivation.

This research lays a foundation for the study of the academic experiences of second-generation Nigerians in the U.S. and further research is needed to generate comprehensive data on this group. As the student population in the United States becomes more diverse, it is imperative that we research the various minority groups to help educators support all children in our schools. Students can succeed in school if we know how best to help them. Despite encountering obstacles, second-generation Nigerian youth in this study performed well in school because several factors came together to empower them to become successful. They were able to navigate the various social contexts to reach their goals.

Notes

Introduction

1. ABC News report about Timi Adelakun, a second-generation Nigerian youth in Florida, as reported by Mariya Moseley, May 14, 2020.
    https://abcnews.go.com/US/high-school-senior-1st-Black-valedictorian-schools-highest/story?id=70693706.

2. Article in Newsday about Jude Okonkwo, a second-generation Nigerian high school graduate of Chaminade High School in New York, April 6, 2017.
    https://www.newsday.com/long-island/education/chaminade-high-school-senior-is-accepted-to-all-ivy-league-schools-1.13373840.

3. ABC News report about Ifeoma White-Thorpe, a second-generation Nigerian youth in New Jersey, as reported by Darla Miles, April 5, 2017.
    https://6abc.com/teenager-ivy-league-college-acceptance/1835305/.

4. NBC News report about Olawunmi Akinlemibola, a second-generation Nigerian youth in Maryland who gained admission into 14 colleges including the following: Emory University, Brown University, University of Chicago, Duke University, Stanford University, Cornell University, Princeton University, Harvard University, and the University of Pennsylvania. April 7, 2017.
    https://www.nbcwashington.com/news/local/prince-georges-county-student-accepted-to-14-colleges.

5. Article in Newsday about Augusta Uwamanzu-Nna, a second-generation Nigerian youth in New York, as reported by Martin C. Evans, May 2, 2016.
https://www.newsday.com/long-island/education/elmont-high-school-s-augusta-uwamanzu-nna-picks-harvard-1.11751476.

6. Article in Boston Globe about Obinna Igbokwe, a second-generation Nigerian in Massachusetts who gained admission into seven Ivy League colleges, as reported by J.D Capelouto, April 27, 2016
https://www.bostonglobe.com/metro/2016/04/27/brockton-high-school-student-gets-into-seven-out-eight-ivy-league-schools/rI3DlHMZPXbEeMxyX8GR5N/story.html.

7. NBC News report about Harold Ekeh, a second-generation Nigerian in New York about his academic feats by Anne Thompson. April 7, 2015.
https://www.nbcnews.com/nightly-news/harold-ekeh-17-long-island-gets-accepted-all-eight-ivy-n337506.

Chapter 1

1. New York Times article by Sara Rimer and Karen Arenson about the overrepresentation of second-generation Africans, including Nigerians and other Black second-generation youth in Ivy League and elite colleges in the United States.
https://www.nytimes.com/2004/06/24/us/top-colleges-take-more-Blacks-but-which- ones.html

June 24, 2004.

Index

Reference

Adeleke, T. (2004). *Critical perspectives on historical and contemporary issues about Africa and Black America.* Lewiston, New York: Edwin Mellen Press.

Ainsworth, J. W. (2002). Why does it take a village? The mediation of neighborhood effects on educational achievement. *Social Forces,* 81(1), 117-152.

Ainsworth-Darnell, J. W., & Downy, D. B. (1998). Assessing the oppositional culture explanation for racial/ethnic differences in school performance. *American Sociological Review, 63,* 536-553.

Aloma, B. O. (2006). Personal and family paths to pupil achievement. *Social Behavior and Personality,* 34(8), 907-922.

Anekwe, P. N. (2008). Characteristics and Challenges of high-achieving second-generation Nigerian youth in the United States. Doctoral dissertation, Western Connecticut State University.

Arthur, J. A. (2000). *Invisible sojourners: African immigrant diaspora in the United States.* Westport, CT: Praeger.

Auerbach, S. (2002). Why do they give the good classes to some and not to others? Latino parent narratives of struggle in a college access program. *Teachers College Record,* 104 (7), 1369-1392.

Bankston, C. (2004). Social capital, cultural values, immigration and academic achievement: The host country context and contradictory consequences. *Sociology of Education,* 77(2), 176-179.

Bankston, C. L., Caldas, S. J., & Zhou, M. (1997). The academic achievement of Vietnamese students: Ethnicity as social capital. *Sociological Focus, 30,* 1-16.

Bandura, A. (1993). Perceived self-efficacy in cognitive development and functioning. *Educational Psychologist, 28*(2), 117-148.

Bandura, A. (2001). Social cognitive theory: An agentic perspective. *Annual Review Psychology, 52,* 1-26.

Booker, S., & Minter, W. (2003). The US and Nigeria: Thinking Beyond oil. Retrieved from http://www.greatdecisions.org.

Bourdieu, P. (1986). The forms of capital. *(pp. 241-258)* In Richardson, J. G. (Ed.). *Handbook of theory and research for Sociology of Education.* New York: Greenwood Press.

Bourhis, R. Y., Montaruli, E., El-Geledi, S., Harvey, & Barrette, S.G. (2010). Acculturation in multiple host community settings. *Journal of Social Issues: Society for the Psychological study of Social Issues,* 66(4),780-8012.

Bowen, N. K., & Bowen, G. L. (1998). The mediating role of educational meaning in the relationship between home academic culture and academic performance. *Family Relations, 47*(1), 45-51.

Bronfenbrenner, U., & Morris, P. (1998). The ecology of developmental process. In W. Damon (Series ed.) and R.M. Lerner (vol. ed.), *Handbook of child psychology: Vol. 1. Theoretical models of human development* (5th ed., pp. 993-1028). New York: Wiley.

Bryce-Laporte, R. S. (1972). Black immigrants: The experience of invisibility and inequality. *Journal of Black Studies, 3*(1), 29-56.

Butcher, K. (1994). Black immigrants in the United States: A comparison with Native Blacks and other immigrants. *Industrial and Labor Relations Review, 47,* 265-284.

Caplan, N., Choy, M. H., & Whitmore, J. K. (1991). *Children of the boat people: A study of educational success.* Ann Arbor: University of Michigan Press.

Chua, A., & Rubenfeld, J. (2014). *The triple package: How unlikely traits explain the rise and fall of cultural groups in America.* New York: Penguin Group.

Cole, D. A. (1991). Preliminary support for a competency-based model of depression in children. *Journal Abnormal Psychology* 100, 181-90.

Coleman, J. S. (1988). Social capital in the creation of human capital. *American Journal of Sociology, 94,* 94-120.

Corbiere, M., Fraccaroli, F., Mbekou, V., & Perron, J. (2006). Academic self-concept and academic interest measurement: A multi-sample European study. *European Journal of Psychology,* 21(1), 3-15.

Dawsey, J. (2018, January 12). Trump derides protections for immigrants from "shithole" countries. The Washington Post. Retrieved from https://www.washingtonpost.com/politics/trump-attacks-protections-for-immigrants-from-shithole-countries-in-oval-office-meeting/2018/01/11/bfc0725c-f711-11e7-91af-31ac729add94_story.html.

Delgado-Gaitan, C. (1991). Involving parents in the schools: A process of empowerment. *American Journal of Education,*100 (1), 20-46.

Delpit, L. D. (1988). The silenced dialogue: Power and pedagogy in educating other people's children. *Harvard Educational Review, 58*(3), 280-298.

Djamba, Y. K. (1999). African immigrants in the United States: A socio-demographic profile in comparison to native Blacks. *Journal of Asian and African Studies,* 34(2), 210-215.

Dodoo, F. N. (1997). Assimilation differences among Africans in America. *Social Forces,* 76, 527-546.

Dodoo, N.F., & Takyi, B. (2002). Africans in the diaspora: Black-White earnings among America's Africans. *Ethnic and Racial Studies,* 25(6), 913-41.

Eccles, J. (1983). Expectations, values, and academic behaviors. In Spence, J. T. (ed.). *Achievement and achievement motives.* San Francisco: W.H. Freeman.

Elliott, J.G., & Bempechat, J. (2002). The culture and contexts of achievement motivation. *New Directions for Child and Adolescent Development,* 96, 7-26.

Ethier, K.A., & Deaux, K. (1994). Negotiating social identity when contexts change: Maintaining identities and responding to threats. *Journal of Personality and Social Psychology,* 67 (2), 243-51.

Fader, M. (2017, July 20). The real first family of hoops. BR Magazine. Retrieved from https://bleacherreport.com/articles/2722400-nneka-chiney-ogwumike.

Fernandez-Kelly, M. P., & Schauffler, R. (1994). Divided fates: Immigrant children in a restructured U.S. economy. *International Migration Review, 28*(4), 662-689.

Fine, M. (1993). Parent involvement: Reflections on parents, power, and urban public schools. *Teachers College Record,* 94 (4), 682-709.

Floyd, C. (1996). Achieving despite the odds: A study of resilience among a group of African American high school seniors. *The Journal of Negro Education, 65*(2), 181-189.

Foley, M. W., & Hoge, D. R. (2007). *Religion and the new immigrants: How faith communities form our newest citizens.* Oxford: Oxford University Press.

Foner, N. (1987). The Jamaicans: Race and ethnicity among migrants in New York. In *New immigrants in New York*, pp. 195-217. New York: Columbia University Press.

Ford, D. Y., Harris, J. J., & Schuerger, J. M. (1993). Racial identity development among gifted Black students: Counseling issues and concerns. *Journal of Development, 71*, 409-417.

Fordham, S. (1988). Racelessness as a factor in Black students' school success: Pragmatic strategy or Pyrrhic victory? *Harvard Education Review*, 56(1), 54-84.

Fordham, S., & Ogbu, J. U. (1986). Black students school success: Coping with the burden of "acting white." *Urban Review, 18*, 176-206.

Foster, K. M. (2004). Coming to terms: A discussion of John Ogbu's cultural-ecological theory of minority academic achievement. *Intercultural Education, 15*(4), 369-384.

Fox, J. (2020, February 5). U.S. could use more Nigerian immigrants. Bloomberg. Retrieved from https://finance.yahoo.com/news/u-could-actually-more-nigerian-133011858.html.

Gibson, M. A. (1988). *Accommodation without assimilation: Punjabi Sikh immigrants in an American high school and community.* Ithaca, N.Y: Cornell University Press.

Gordon, M. (1964). *Assimilation in American life.* New York: Oxford University Press.

Goyette, K. U., & Xie, Y. (1999). Educational expectations of Asian American youth: Determinants and ethnic differences. *Sociology of Education, 72,* 22-36.

Grieco, E. (2004). The African foreign born in the United States. *Migration Policy Institute.* Retrieved from https://www. migrationpolicy.org/article/african-foreign-born-united-states-2002.

Griffin, L. J., & Alexander, K. (1978). Schooling and socio-economic attainment: High school and college influence. *American Journal of Sociology* 84, 319-47.

Habecker, S. (2017). Becoming African Americans: African immigrant youth in the United States and hybrid assimilation. *Africology: The Journal of Pan African Studies,* 10 (1), 55-75.

Hagopian, A., Thompson, M. J., Fordyce, M., Johnson, K. E., & Hart, G. (2004). The migration of physicians from Sub-Saharan Africa to the United States of America: Measures of the brain drain. *Human Resource Health, 2*(17). Retrieved from http://www. pubmedcentral.nih.gov/articlerender.fcgi?artid=5444595.

Hao, L., & Bonstead-Bruns, M. (1998). Parent-child differences in educational expectations and the academic achievement of immigrant and native students. *Sociology of Education,* 71(3), 175-198.

Hayes, K. (1992). Attitudes toward education: Voluntary and involuntary immigrants from the same families. *Anthropology and Education Quarterly, 23*(3), 250-267.

Hernandez, D. (2012). Changing demography and circumstances for young Black children in African and Caribbean immigrant families. Migration Policy Institute: Washington, DC.

Herrnstein, R., & Murray, C. (1994). *The bell curve: Intelligence and class structure in American life.* New York: Free Press.

Ianni, F. A. J. (1989). *The search for structure: A report on American youth today.* New York: Free Press.

Jacob, E., & Jordan, C. (1987). Explaining the school performance of minority students. *Anthropology and Education Quarterly, 18*(4), 259-61.

Jacobs, J. E., & Eccles, J. S. (1992). The impact of mothers' gender role stereotypic beliefs on mothers' and children's' ability perceptions. *Journal of Personality Sociology and Psychology, 63,*932-44.

Kao, G., (1995). Asian-Americans as model minorities? A look at their academic performance. *American Journal of Education, 103,* 121-159.

Kao, G. (2004). Social capital and its relevance to minority and immigrant populations. *Sociology of Education, 77,* 172-183.

Kao, G., & Tienda, M. (1995). Optimism and achievement: The educational performance of immigrant youth. *Social Science Quarterly, 76*(1), 1-19.

Kao, G., & Tienda, M. (1998). Educational aspirations of minority youth. *American Journal of Education, 106,* 349-384.

Kao, G., & Rutherford, L. T. (2007). Does social capital still matter? Immigrant minority disadvantage in school-specific social capital and its effects on academic achievement. *Sociological Perspectives, 50*(1), 27-52.

Kao, G., & Thompson, J. S. (2003). Racial and ethnic stratification in educational achievement and attainment. *Annual Review Sociology, 29*, 417-442.

Kent, M. M. (2007). Immigration and America's Black Population. *Population Bulletin, 62*(4).

Kibria, N. (2002). Of blood, belonging as homeland trips: Transnational and identity among second-generation Chinese and Korean Americans. In *The changing faces of home: The Transnational lives of the second-generation*, edited by Peggy Levitt and Mary C. Waters. New York: Russell Sage Foundation.

Kim, R. Y. (2002). Ethnic differences in academic achievement between Vietnamese and Cambodian children: Cultural and structural explanations. *The Sociological Quarterly, 43*(2), 213-35.

Kindermann, T. A. (1993). Natural peer groups as contexts for individual development: The case of children's motivation in school. *Developmental Psychology, 29*, 970-77.

Kposowa, A. J. (2002). Human capital and the performance of African immigrants in the U.S. labor market" *The Western Journal of Black Studies, 26* (3),175-83.

LeVine, R. A. (1966). *Dreams and deeds: Achievement motivation in Nigeria.* Chicago: The University of Chicago Press.

Li, J. (2004). Parental expectations of immigrants: A folk theory about children's school achievement. *Race Ethnicity and Education, 7*(2), 167-183.

Lobo, A. P. (2001). U.S. Diversity Visas are Attracting Africa's Best and Brightest. *Population Today, 29*(5).

Logan, J., & Deane, G. (2003). Black diversity in Metropolitan America Report, Lewis Mumford Center, University at Albany, State University of New York. Retrieved from http://mumford1.dyndns.or/cen2000/report.html.

Massey, D. S., Mooney, M., Torres, K. C., & Charles, C. Z. (2007). Black immigrants and Black Natives attending selective colleges and universities in the United States. *American Journal of Education, 113*, 243-271.

Matute-Bianchi, M. (1986). Ethnic identities and patterns of school success and failure among Mexican-Descent and Japanese American students in a California high school: An ethnographic analysis. *American Journal of Education, 95*(1), 233-255.

Meece, J. L., & Kurtz-Costes, B. (2001). Introduction: The schooling of ethnic minority children and youth. *Educational Psychologist, 36*(1), 1-7.

Meyers, B., Dowdy, J. & Paterson, P. (2000). Finding the missing voices: Perspectives of the least visible families and their willingness and capacity for school involvement. *Current Issues in Middle Level Education* 7 (2), 59-79.

Miller, L. P., & Tanners, L. A. (1995). Diversity and the new immigrants. *Teachers College Record, 96*(4), 671-680.

Mittelberg, D., & Waters, M.C. (1992). The process of ethnogenesis among Haitian and Israeli immigrants in the United States. *Ethnic and Racial Studies*, 15(3), 412-435.

Model, S., & Ladipo, D. (1996). Context and Opportunity: Minorities in London and New York. *Social Forces*, 75, 485-510.

O'Connor, C., Lewis, A., & Mueller, J. (2007). Researching 'Black' educational experiences and outcomes: Theoretical and methodological considerations. *Educational Researcher*, 36 (9), 541-52.

Ogbu, J. U. (1978). *Minority education and caste: The American system in cross-cultural perspective*. New York: Academic Press.

Ogbu, J. U. (1982). Cultural discontinuities and schooling. *Anthropology and Education Quarterly*, *13*(4), 290-307.

Ogbu, J. U. (1987). Variability in minority school performance: A problem in search of an exploration. *Anthropology and Education Quarterly*, *18*(4), 312-334.

Ogbu, J. U. (1991). Immigrant and involuntary minorities in comparative perspective. In M. Gibson & J. Ogbu (Eds.) *Minorities' status and schooling: A comparative study of immigrant and involuntary minorities*. New York: Garland Press.

Ogbu, J. U. (1992). Understanding cultural diversity and learning. *Educational Researcher*, *21*(8), 5-14.

Ogbu, J. U. (1993). Differences in cultural frames of reference. *International Journal of Behavioral Development*, *16*(3), 483-506.

Ogbu, J. U. (2004). Collective identity and the burden of "acting white" in Black history, community, and education. *The Urban Review, 36*(1), 1-35.

Ogbu, J. U., & Matute-Bianchi, M. E. (1986). Understanding sociocultural factors: Knowledge, identity, and school adjustment. In California State Department of Education (Ed.), *Beyond language: Social and cultural factors in schooling language minority students* (pp. 73-142) Los Angeles: CA State Department of Education, Evaluation, Dissemination, and Assessment Center.

Ojiaku, O., & Ulansky, G. (1972). Early Nigerian response to American education. *Phylon, 33*(4), 380-88.

Okagaki, L. (2001). Triarchic model of minority children's school achievement. *Educational Psychologist, 36*(1), 9-20.

Omoyibo, K. U. (2002). *Adolescent females' reproductive health in Nigeria: A study on the legislation and socio-cultural impediments to abortion an against female circumcision.* New York: Peter Lang.

Onwujuba, C., & Marks, L. (2015). Why we do what we do: Reflections of educated Nigerian immigrants on their changing parenting attitudes and practices. *Family Science Review, 20* (2).

Oyserman, D., Harrison, K., & Bybee, D. (2001). Can racial identity be promotive of academic efficacy? *International Journal of Behavioral Development, 25*(4), 379-385.

Pajares, F. (2003). Self-efficacy beliefs, motivation, and achievement in writing: A review of the literature. *Reading and Writing Quarterly, 19,* 139-158.

Parcel, T. L., & Dufur, M. J. (2001). Capital at home and school: Effects on student achievement. *Social Forces, 79*(3), 881-911.

Park, R. E. (1928). Human migration and the marginal man. *American Journal of Sociology,* 33, 881-893.

Parsons, J. E., Terry, G., Adler, T. G., & Kaczala, C. (1982). Socialization of achievement attitudes and beliefs: Parental influences. *Child Development,* 53,310-21.

Phelan, P., Davidson, A. L., & Yu, H. C. (1993). Students' multiple worlds: Navigating the borders of family, peer, and school cultures. In P. Phelan & A. L. Davidson (Eds.), *Renegotiating cultural diversity in American schools,* (pp. 52-88). New York: Teachers College Press.

Phinney, J. S. (1990). Ethnic identity in adolescents and adults: Reviews of research. *Psychological Bulletin,* 10, 499-514.

Portes, A. (1996a). *The new second generation.* New York: Russell Sage Foundation.

Portes, A., & MacLeod, D. (1996). Educational progress of children of immigrants: The roles of class, ethnicity, and school context. *Sociology of Education,* 69 (4): 255-75.

Portes, A., MacLeod, S.A., & Park, R. N. (1978). Immigrant aspirations. *Sociology of Education, 51*(4), 241-260.

Portes, A., & Rumbaut, R. G. (1996). *Immigrant America: A portrait.* (Rev. Ed.). Berkeley: University of California Press.

Portes, A., & Rumbaut, R. G. (2001). *Legacies: The story of the immigrant second generation.* Berkeley: University of California Press.

Portes, A., & Zhou, M. (1993). The new second generation: Segmented assimilation and its variants. *Annals of the American Political and Social Sciences, 530*, 74-96.

Portes, P. R. (1996b). Ethnicity and culture in educational psychology. In D.C. Berliner & R. C. Calfee (Eds.), *Handbook of educational psychology* (pp. 331-357). New York: Macmillan.

Portes, P.R. (1999). Social and psychological factors in the academic achievement of children of immigrants: A cultural historical puzzle. *American Educational Research Journal, 36*(3), 489-507.

Raudenbush, S., & Bryk, A. S. (1989). A multilevel model of the social distribution of high school achievement. *Sociology of Education, 62*, 172-92.

Reis, M., & Diaz, E. (1999). Economically disadvantaged urban female students who achieve in schools. *The Urban Review, 31*(1), 31-56.

Rhamie, J., & Hallam, S. (2002). An investigation into African-Caribbean academic success in the UK. *Race Ethnicity and Education, 5*(2).

Rimer, S., & Arenson, K. (2004). Top colleges take more Blacks, but which ones? *The New York Times.* Retrieved from http://www.nytimes.com/2004/06/24/education/24AFFI.final.html?pag.

Roberts, S. (2005). More Africans enter US than in days of slavery. *The New York Times* Retrieved from http://www.nytimes.com/2005/02/21/nyregion/21africa.htm.

Rumbaut, R.G. (1994a). The crucible within: Ethnic identity, self-esteem and segmented assimilation among children of immigrants. *International Migration Review, 8*, 748-794.

Rumbaut, R. G. (1994b). Origins and destinies: Immigration to the U.S. since WWII. *Sociological Forum, 9*(4), 583-622.

Sears, D. O., Fu, M., Henry, P.J., & Bui, K. (2003). The origins and persistence of ethnic identity among the new immigrant groups. *Social Psychology Quarterly,* 66 (4), 419-37.

Sharma, H. L., & Nasa, N. (2014). Academic self-efficacy: A reliable predictor of educational performances. *British Journal of Education,* 2 (3), 57-64.

Slaughter-Defoe, D. T., Nakagawa, K., Takanishi, R., & Johnson, D. J. (1990). Toward cultural/ecological perspectives on schooling and achievement in African-and Asian-American children. *Child Development, 61,* 363-383.

Smith, W. (2008). How does membership in Irish organizations contribute to ethnic identity? *Virginia Social Science Journal,* 43, 56-75.

Spencer, M. B., Cole, S. P., Dupree, D., Glymph, A., & Pierre, P. (1993). Self-efficacy among urban African American early adolescents: Exploring issues of risk, vulnerability, and residence. *Developmental Psychology, 5,* 719-739.

Stanton-Salazar, R. D. (1997). A social capital framework for understanding the socialization of racial minority children and youth. *Harvard Educational Review, 67*(1), 1-40.

Sue, S., & Okazaki, S. (1990). Asian-American educational achievements: A phenomenon in search of an explanation. *American Psychologist, 45*(8), 913-920.

Suzuki, R. H. (1980). Education and socialization of Asian Americans: A revisionist analysis of the "model minority" thesis. In R. Endo, S. Sue, and N. N. Wagner (Eds.). *Asian-Americans: Social and psychological perspective*, vol. 2, 155-175.

Szalacha, L. A., Marks, A. K., Lamarre, M., & Garcia Coll, C. (2005). Academic pathways and children of immigrant families. *Research in Human Development*, 2(4), 179- 211.

Takougang, J. (1995). Recent African immigrants to the United States: A historical perspective. *The Western Journal of Black Studies*, *19*(1), 50-57.

Takyi, B. K. (2002). The making of the second diaspora: On the recent African immigrant community in the United States of America. *The Western Journal of Black Studies*, *26*(1), 32-43.

Tatum, B. D. *(1992)*. Talking about race, learning about racism: The Application of racial identity development theory in the classroom. *Harvard Educational Review,* 62 (1).

Teachman, J. D. (1987). Family background, educational resources, and educational attainment. *American Sociological Review*, *52*(4), 548-557.

Traore, R. L. (2003). African students in America: Reconstructing new meanings of "African American" in urban education. *Intercultural Education,* 14(3), 243-54.

Trueba, H. T. (1991). Comments on Foley's "Reconsidering anthropological explanations." *Anthropology and Education Quarterly,* *22*(1), 87-94.

Ukpokodu, O., (2017). African immigrant children, families and U.S. PK-12 Schools. *In Erasing invisibility, inequality, and social justice of Africans in the diaspora and the continent* (1st ed.) edited by Omiunota Ukpokodu and Peter Ojambo. UK: Cambridge Scholars Publishing.

Vickerman, M. (1999). *Crosscurrents: West Indian immigrants and race.* New York: Oxford University Press.

Vickerman, M. (2001). Jamaicans: Balancing race and ethnicity. In Nancy Foner (Ed.), *New immigrants in New York* (revised and updated edition), pp. 201-228. New York: Columbia University Press.

Villenas, S., & Deyhle, D. (1999). Critical race theory and ethnographies challenging the stereotypes: Latino families, schooling, resilience, and resistance. *Curriculum Inquiry,* 29 (4), 413-445.

Wagner, B., & Phillips, D. (1992). Beyond beliefs: Parent and child behaviors and children's perceived academic competence. *Child Development,* 63, 1150-1391.

Walker, B. (2003). The cultivation of students' self-efficacy in reading and writing. *Reading and Writing Quarterly, 19,* 173-187.

Waters, M.C. (1990). *Ethnic options: Choosing identities in America.* Berkeley: University of California Press.

Waters, M. (1994). Ethnic and racial identities of second-generation Black immigrants in New York City. *International Migration Review, 28,* 795-820.

Waters, M. (1999). *Black identities*: *West Indian immigrant dreams and American realities*. Cambridge, MA: Harvard University Press.

Zephir, F. (2001). *Trends in ethnic identification among second-generation Haitian immigrants in New York City*. Westport, CT: Bergin and Garvey.

Zhou, M. (1997). Growing up American: The challenges confronting immigrant children and children of immigrants. *Annual Review of Sociology*, *23*, 63-95.

Zhou, M., & Bankston, C. L. (1998*). Growing up American: How Vietnamese children adapt to life in the United States*. New York: Russell Sage Foundation.

www.ingramcontent.com/pod-product-compliance
Lightning Source LLC
Chambersburg PA
CBHW030240030426
42336CB00009B/189